T0386782

'*The Motherhood Space* is a beautiful dive into the depths and realities of modern-day mothering. Gabrielle weaves stories and wisdom together to create a place for women to land that speaks of the complexities and beauty of parenting. You won't feel alone reading this book.'

LAEL STONE

'For years I believed that no one was talking about what *really* happens to a woman when she becomes a mother. But I was wrong. People were talking about it – many experts and wise women with insights we *should* have all had – they just weren't accessible to a new mama like me. Gabrielle has beautifully pulled together all those experts and insights, plus stories of mamas' experiences, and finally made it accessible for us all.'

AMY TAYLOR-KABBAZ

The Motherhood Space

A companion through the beautiful chaos of life as a modern mother

By Gabrielle Nancarrow

The Motherhood Space

A companion through the beautiful chaos of life as a modern mother

By Gabrielle Nancarrow

Hardie Grant

BOOKS

For Bell and for Moni.

You are in the depths of new motherhood
and I am watching you in awe.

Feel it all. Trust yourself. Call me any time.

And for James.

None of this, without you.

What? You too?
I thought I was the only one.

CS Lewis

Contents

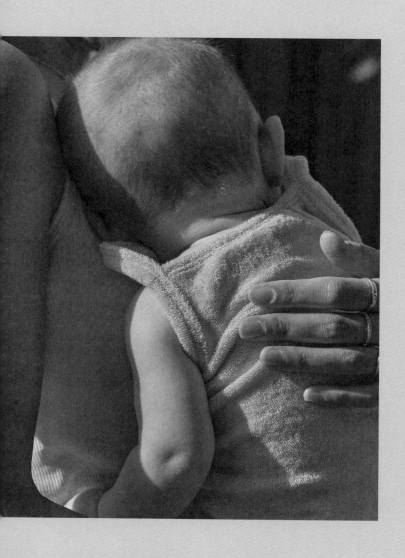

Before we begin   9
Introduction   10

Cultivating

Ready, or not   17
Choices   23
Longing and loss   33
Pregnancy and birth   43
Birth trauma   60

Tending

The first forty days   67
Pelvic care   78
Maiden to mother   81
Intuition   90
Feeding   99
Sleep   109

Growing

Loneliness and finding
time to be alone   120
Firsts, lasts and letting go   125
Slow days and simple joys   134
Surrendering to
the chaos   141
Another baby?   144

Honouring

Motherhood, feminism
and the patriarchy   152
The mental, emotional,
invisible load   168
Motherhood rage   179
Matrescence and identity   183
Friendships and
community   199
Relationships, intimacy
and sexuality   209
Our bodies, self-care
and rest   219
Anxiety and depression   223
Guilt and being enough   229
Mothering outside the
nuclear narrative   236
Imprints and healing
our wounds   245
Mothering without mothers   250
Creating space and staying
close   255
Feeling lost and feeling
found   261

A note to my children   265
Thank you   268
About the author   271

Before we begin

I acknowledge that I write from a position of immense privilege. I am a white, middle-class woman living in Australia. I have not experienced racism or poverty. I have always been free to make decisions about my body and my uterus. I have been supported by my partner and my family throughout my pregnancies, births and postpartum journeys, and have had some paid government parental leave on the two occasions I birthed in Australia (although Australia has one of the least generous government parental leave programs in the developed world).

What I have set out to capture in these pages is a breadth of motherhood experience that goes beyond my own, inviting many voices into the conversation. Mothers do the world's most important work and yet it remains invisible, unsupported and unpaid. My hope for this book, beyond providing comfort in our shared experiences, is to further the conversation of how unacceptably challenging it is to parent in a culture that does not acknowledge or value the work of motherhood or the importance of raising the next generation of humans.

I hope everyone who reads this book who identifies as a mother – whether you are straight, LGBTQIA+, living with a disability, Indigenous, white, black, brown, childless, or are a solo, step, single, partnered or adoptive mother – feel honoured and included in the narrative and the stories. It is often only those parenting within the bounds of the heteronormative nuclear narrative who feel seen and represented in books. I hope that whatever your story, you feel included here.

Finally, I acknowledge the Wurundjeri People of the Kulin Nation who are the original and true custodians of the land on which this book was conceived, written and created. I pay my respects to Elders past and present.

Introduction

This book was written in the notes on my phone, on torn pieces of paper around my home and from conversations that have been swimming around in my head since I finished my first book *The Birth Space* a few years ago. I knew there was so much more to unearth about the motherhood experience, and it felt like both the best time in my life and the worst time in my life to pursue such a project. The best time, because I am so deep in it – my children are eight, five and two. And the worst time, because I am so deep in it. I didn't have the time to write this book but the pull of it wouldn't leave me. It clung to my consciousness like my toddler clings to my leg as I shuffle around the house and I will be forever grateful that it did because as mothers, we need our stories shared – indeed, we need them shouted. The wonder, the rage, the beauty, the fear, the grief, the hugeness of it all needs to be validated and honoured and revered and reckoned with. This book felt necessary, and while it took me away from my children for days and nights on end, I knew I had to do it.

In the beginning, as I planned these pages, my thoughts were often scrambled and always fleeting. Words and sentences that occasionally made sense were jotted down mid-bathtime or in the early morning hours before everyone else woke up – before my brain felt fried for the day at 7.30 am. Finding space to work and to create amidst the overwhelm and chaos of motherhood is an everyday challenge that was more real to me this year, writing this book, than it has ever been. I spent weeks arranging and rearranging the structure of what follows here. I initially thought there would be a neat chronology, a tidy sequence to the chapters beginning with pregnancy and birth and moving through the years. But as I got further into it, that started to make less sense. Motherhood isn't neat, and so, I figured, a book about motherhood shouldn't be, either. Our thoughts and emotions bleed into one another, overlapping and crashing like waves on a wild day, coming and going, showing up in moments when we least expect it, taking our breath away. Who knew it was possible to move from joy to rage so swiftly? Not I, until I became a mother.

So while the structure here is fairly loose, my intent for this book has always been firm: an honouring of the motherhood experience. A truth-telling. A reflection on the seasons that, while fleeting, feel never-ending when we are living them. A book that I wish existed when I was pregnant for the first time, on the cusp of something I knew was big, yet I did not have the words to articulate what I was feeling and moving through and also, waiting for.

So much of what we do and feel as mothers is impossible to put into words – it is a knowing that cannot be known until it is lived. But as I have grown in this role, a language of sorts has slowly formed, and this is what I have come up with so far: motherhood is a delicate unravelling of self and a reckoning with all that I thought I knew. It is filled to the brim with magic. It's an invitation to play again. It's never being alone. It's joy entwined with grief entwined with fear. It's a constant and painful lesson in letting go and letting my children be, and a deep knowing that I have little control over this journey and of what is unfolding before me. It's that familiar tension of needing space but never wanting to be without them. It's knowing and remembering the gentle weight of their newborn body asleep in my arms and the ache that comes when they grow and I realise I may never feel that again. It's sacrifices, big and small. It's teaching and learning. It's all-consuming self-doubt. It's being saved by being heard. It's a daily fight against the patriarchy that wants to control our bodies, our pregnancies and our births and expects us to mother unsupported, and without recognition or value. It's a mirror and a time machine. It's a spiritual journey and the ultimate lesson in surrender. It's lying next to my children at night telling stories and scratching backs and wishing they would fall asleep and then staying there a little bit longer when they finally do. Above all else, it is fierce, gentle, unconditional love.

Halfway through writing this book, I went to stay with my mum and dad for a week on my own in my childhood home on the Victorian coast. No children. No distractions. I missed them, but I also found the mental and physical space I needed to write uninterrupted. When our children are close by, I am never alone. I actually think the moment we start longing for a child we are never truly alone again, our minds consumed with love and worry. That week, I allowed myself to be mothered. My mum brought me food and tea and hugs and the morning walks we took, arm-in-arm, were so grounding. Since becoming a mother I haven't had many opportunities to be present with my parents – it's always so busy and loud with our children around, a chaos I welcome but which means I am often preoccupied. That week I soaked up every single precious minute of being with them and being cared for by them. We all need to be mothered by someone. It is our life force.

In the pages that follow, I share my own journey of motherhood alongside the voices of more than fifty women. These women are anthropologists, sociologists, psychologists, midwives, sexologists, teachers, doctors, parenting and relationship experts, writers, artists, photographers, models, consultants, creatives and doulas. Some are mothers and some are not and their wisdom and insights moved me beyond measure. Their words feel like an antidote to the stories we grew up with, the ones that brought with them expectations and shame and guilt and the weight of the 'good mother' narrative. The truth is, loving our children is the easy part. It's mothering under the patriarchy that drowns us. I hope our voices help you to see that you are doing an incredible job against all the odds, and that you are not alone in what you are feeling.

The conversations I had with these women, and the themes I drew from them for the chapters in this book, feel at once universal and deeply personal: what is it to mother and do I even want to be a mother? The intersection of motherhood, feminism and the patriarchy. Our shifting identity. The tender ache that comes with the passing of time. The fight to hold on to the relationships that mean the most to us. Our sexuality. Our strength. Our bodies. Our minds. Our emotions and tending to the emotions of those we hold dear. The long nights and very early mornings. The crazy love and utter chaos of raising children. The tug of war that is career and mothering and searching for ourselves and for equality amidst it all.

My sincere hope for this book is that you read these pages – hopefully in the bath without an audience, but more likely in the stolen moments throughout your days and nights – and feel less alone. I know I cannot shine a light on every one of our journeys – there are as many experiences of motherhood as there are mothers in the world. I hope that by surfacing some of our stories and capturing as much as possible what motherhood feels like – the joy and the pain, the ordinary and the extraordinary – that these pages speak to you. I hope that you will be able to turn to any page in this book at any point in your motherhood journey and feel seen and heard and held and loved and acknowledged and validated for all you do and for all you are. In a world where community and support are not all that easy to find, I hope you find it here.

My love to you, beautiful mother. You are doing an extraordinary job.

Cultivating

Motherhood is an invitation into the unknown. It is a spiritual quest and a rite of passage like no other. Before any of that, though, it is a feeling, a knowing, a plan, a dream, an ache, sometimes a surprise, occasionally a long journey. This is the season of cultivation – everything that comes before the birth of your baby. It is a season of promise, hope and awe, and it might also be one of loss and pain and fear. It is a season rich with beauty and growth and change and questions. Endless questions. Questions like, *Do I want to become a mother? Am I ready? How will it change me? How will it change us? How do I want to birth? How do I want to mother?* It is a season that will take you all the way to the very edge of your limits and show you that you are stronger than you ever thought possible. And it is a season that you will return to each time you long for, conceive, grow, birth and mother a child. It is the season of beginnings and the birth of you as a mother.

There is so much love and grief in being a mother.

"

Kara Hoppe
Psychotherapist, author, teacher and
mother of Jude and Dion

Ready, or not

Knowing the right time to have a baby, or another baby, or even knowing if a baby is right for you, is one of the most personal decisions a woman can make.

You might have a deep sense that motherhood is and has always been something you want, or don't want. Or maybe you are coming to an age that society – and every relative and doctor – tells you is your scary fertility age and you must get pregnant now or else, but you're not ready or you don't have a partner and you don't want to do it on your own or your career is taking off or you're just not feeling the urge or there are other reasons why it's not the right time. Perhaps you're wrestling with some big questions that are important to consider before you start trying to conceive like, *Why am I choosing this path? What kind of parent do I want to be? Am I with the right partner? Do I have support? Can I afford a baby? Do I want to do this on my own? How will a child change the course of my career? How many children would I like to have? Am I ready for this?*

Whatever the answers to these questions, they're all valid. Your life will have beauty in it no matter which path you choose to take or which one unfolds before you. Sometimes we have to remind ourselves of that, such is the noise surrounding us.

I remember the moment I knew I wasn't ready for a baby, yet. We were living in New York and had flown to San Francisco for Thanksgiving. It was 2012 and I'd been bringing up the idea of babies for more than a year. In that dimly lit hotel room in the Mission District, just about to head out for dinner, my husband James turned to me and said, out of the blue and a little too casually, 'I'm ready. Let's do it. Let's have a baby.' I stood there, shocked. Not so much by his words but by my reaction to them. Instead of being excited like I thought I would be, I felt anxious, and a little dizzy. I was not at all ready, anymore. How could I be? How could anyone ever be ready to step into the greatest unknown there is? I had a career I loved and a life I loved and so many plans and all of a sudden, as much as I wanted to be a mother, nothing added up anymore. How could I, how would I, balance it all? Notice the 'I'? I wasn't thinking 'we' – how would *we* balance it all? The societal weight and expectation that women must be able to work and mother and make it all look effortless was very real to me at that moment and we hadn't even conceived yet.

I told James I wasn't ready – at the very least I needed to take prenatal vitamins for a few months, didn't I? I thought that would buy me time while I figured out where my head was at. I was thirty, we were married, and babies were the next step according to the heteronormative cultural narrative we grew up with. But I knew I wasn't ready and I wanted to sit with that for a while.

We are cracked wide open at some point in our mothering journey and it is then that we must surrender to the experience, as painful as it can be. It can happen early, in the preconception or conception phase, if pregnancy doesn't come easily or there is a loss or multiple losses, or we're feeling pressure to have a child but aren't yet ready and have to work hard to drown out a lifetime of conditioning to figure out what we really want. Sometimes it happens during pregnancy if pregnancy is not what we expected it to be, and it ends up being so hard we don't know if we could ever do it again, even though we longed for more than one child. It often happens during birth or in the days just before birth, when we must truly let go and stop resisting whatever has been holding us back, when we must clear the blocks and soften to the experience.

The Motherhood Space

In my work as a doula, I feel such privilege sitting in this space with women and holding them as they move through to the other side. I once supported a woman who, towards the end of her labour, looked up at me and said, 'I need you to tell me I am going to be a good mother.' She wanted to hear it from someone outside of herself – she wanted to know she could do this monumental thing. I told her that I believed she would be an incredible mother, but what I thought wasn't really what mattered. I told her she needed to believe it herself, to go deep and wrestle with whatever was holding her back from believing it to be true.

I think if we get all the way to postpartum without cracking then the early days and weeks and months and sometimes even years of parenthood can be more painful than we could ever have imagined. Whenever it is, we have to crack. It is the only way through.

I cracked early. After sitting with the idea of motherhood for a few months and wading through a hectic internal monologue of *Am I ready? What does ready feel like? What if I can't get pregnant? What if I lose everything I have worked for? Should we even be bringing a baby into this crazy world? What if I miss my old life? What if I never sleep again? What if it breaks us?* I eventually found myself being drawn towards the *What if it's wonderful?* thoughts, and told James one February night in 2013, a few months after that conversation on Thanksgiving. We were sitting at the bar at Rubirosa in Nolita, our favourite neighbourhood restaurant where we went every Friday night. I remember it was snowing outside and I had this sudden vision of sitting in the exact same spot with our bundled-up newborn one year later. I'm not usually one to manifest but the vision was strong and so I said to him, just as casually as he'd said to me three months earlier, 'I think I'm ready.'

I fell pregnant easily and we spent the next five weeks walking around New York with the greatest little secret growing inside me. I was nervous about the chaos I knew would ensue when we brought our little New Yorker home to our studio apartment, but in those few short weeks of my very first pregnancy, everything felt right.

I had an ultrasound at eight weeks and our baby was measuring small and didn't yet have a heartbeat. I was told that our dates must be off and to come back a week later. In my blissful naivety I thought everything was fine, so much so that I told James not to worry about coming to the next ultrasound. A week later I was back and just as our baby appeared on the screen I was told matter-of-factly that they still did not have a heartbeat and that my pregnancy was not viable. I became a mother in that moment. A heartbroken one. Mourning our baby due in February. Who was meant to be bundled up at the bar with us. Our baby that we loved and who had become such a part of us in the few weeks we knew of their existence. Our baby I felt was with us then and I feel is still with us today. Sometimes I even see them playing alongside our other three children. Is that strange? Maybe. But I see them there. Ever present.

The experience of losing our first baby taught me early on that nothing in parenthood is a given. As much as we want to protect our children, we cannot, and that is the scariest thing in the world. When I became pregnant with our daughter just a few months later, I felt both happiness and fear, knowing how quickly it could all be over. And even though my head was telling me to be cautious, I fell immediately in love with her. We were staying at the beach when I found out I was pregnant for the second time and I remember waking early, doing the test, and then walking down to the water while James slept. I watched the sunrise and felt the presence of both our children, the one who was with us for just a moment and the one I hoped would stay with us for a lifetime. As I write this, our eight-year-old daughter, Camille, is bouncing around outside playing *Harry Potter* with her little sister Audrey. She is a force of creativity and imagination and colour. When she was born, I felt myself exhale. I hadn't realised I had been holding my breath for nine months.

JESSIE'S STORY

This sounds so completely ridiculous, but I'm almost in shock at how suddenly this all seems to have happened. I'm struck by the biological inequality of it all. Up until age thirty, I felt like I could live like a man. Now, I'm struck with this sense of urgency that no man my age could ever relate to. They have all the time in the world. I feel unreasonable anger when I see men decide at fifty-five that they would like to be a dad, and then settle down with a woman twenty-five years younger and it all looks so easy. Women don't get that luxury.

The expectations don't bother me so much, because I know I want babies, but I probably don't need people reminding me that my fertility has a time limit because I am already very aware. I feel enormous anxiety. My career has more momentum than it ever has, and I love it. I've been socialised for thirty-one years to hustle and work and climb and say 'yes' and all of a sudden, the message is to press pause. My brain can't recalibrate.

I've been saying 'in the next year' for a few years. I know that if I want a few children, I need to get started. Maybe it's my industry, which can be so 'gig' based, but I have a sense that if I step back for a period I'll be forgotten, then replaced, and I will have lost all that momentum. Men of the same age continue to rise, while their babies are born and cared for. I'm not resentful towards my partner or men in general, because I know biologically I have to be the one to give birth and if I want to breastfeed that's a whole other thing. It makes sense for me to be the primary carer, at least for a while. And I'm excited about caring for someone and for the level of meaning I think motherhood will offer me – a purpose beyond my career.

I am also terrified – of being overwhelmed and of sleep deprivation. Of the chaos. The mess. The lack of control. I'm worried about being a bad mother or a lazy mother. I haven't even had a baby and I'm terrified about something happening to them. I'm worried about how my work will suffer. That I'll never be the same. I am worried I won't be as ambitious or focused and that my twenties will feel like a dream that I'm desperate to get back. I worry too – if I'm being completely honest – that I'll have a baby and think, 'I should never have done this'. That it will throw everything I love about my life into utter disarray, and it will be the biggest mistake I ever make. The depth of feelings when it comes to kids seems like a lot.

When I think about motherhood the first words that come to mind are responsibility, patience, tenderness and adoration. But actually, before any of that, comes a feeling I find almost impossible to explain. It's something so far beyond connection and I am yearning for it. Motherhood is a level of selflessness that I, as a woman who doesn't have children but hopes to one day, cannot begin to imagine. There is so much about it that seems unknowable.

Jessie Stephens, author

Choices

As women, we absorb cultural messages – some would say pressure – to become mothers.

From the moment we're given our first doll, we're expected to nurture it, naturally. Some of us thrive in this role and others don't. Some will choose this path while others won't. Some will want it desperately but won't be able to have it and for others, it will be thrust upon them. The one guarantee is that every woman will have to contend with the questions and the expectations: *When are you having babies? How many are you going to have? When are you having your next baby? Are you done having babies? Why haven't you had a baby yet?* As if it's anyone else's business but our own.

KAYLA'S STORY

Last year I turned thirty-three. It was another year where I thought I'd be a mother and yet did not try to be. Well-meaning friends often tell me that there is no 'right' time to have a baby, but I know intuitively that I'm not quite ready yet. I'm still tending to the dense forest of my life, creating a clearing to birth a baby in – a quieter, softer space where I've spent time preparing and meeting the deeply human parts of me.

I'm finding that this process takes time, and while I've been in this liminal space, the pace of time around me seems different. I've witnessed friends become pregnant and birth and raise their newborns, magnificently blooming into an expanded version of themselves. I've noticed the shift in tone from the people around me. My family, who once made subtle comments to sense my intentions of having kids, now ask pointed and probing questions. My doctor no longer indulges my remarks that 'I've got plenty of time', instead reminding me of the statistics of birthing after thirty-five. Even my social media feed betrays my unhurried approach by promoting baby products.

On some days it all feels too much. It's loud and fast and urgent. On those days, I remind myself that a seed needs fertile soil to grow into a plant that thrives. We don't question its need for space and the right conditions to grow with the season – we create it and allow it to be, and watch and wait. It's this kind of environment that I'm cultivating – one that feels luxuriously slow and tender, in a world that's demanding us to be otherwise.

I sense this approach will be important for me too, in those early days and months of motherhood. To genuinely unlearn the productivity-oriented habits that I've cultivated over thirty-plus years and the association that society has conditioned between my output and my worth, by leaning into a period of life with a newborn that focuses on being rather than doing. Where the passage of time is marked by moments of sleep and feeding, changes to their soft downy hair, the appearance of new facial expressions, and the space for me to appreciate the marvel of it all as it unfolds.

Kayla Robertson, mental health practitioner and mindfulness facilitator

There is an energetic, emotional and physical activation that happens when we become a mother – an activation of the womb energy in the centre of a woman's body. This activation happens when we give birth and it can also happen when we adopt or however we step into the role of mother. Every woman has access to their womb energy, which is a source of creativity and also a portal where we can access medicine and guidance, yet not every woman feels welcome in this space. For those who have not birthed it can feel like there is a boundary around it, a limitation. Living from our womb wisdom is deeply healing and if we removed these limitations it would benefit so many women.

"

Tami Lynn Kent
Author of *Wild Creative, Wild Feminine* and *Mothering From Your Center*, and mother of three sons

GRACE'S STORY

One of my earliest memories is playing at kindergarten with a classmate. It's a cold morning, and my friend is telling me with big wide eyes that when we grow up we will have to marry boys so we can have babies. Boys?! I was shocked. 'No way,' was my reply. 'I'm going to marry a girl.' Her response was flat, and matter-of-fact, 'You're not allowed to, it's illegal.' And just like that, my life is laid out before me. I will grow up. I will marry a boy. I will have babies. It's a narrative that is repeated to me throughout my childhood. In books and TV shows, in the role models around me, in the passing 'one day when you're a mum' comments.

As I got older, the prospect of having kids was no longer a dim, distant suggestion, but something that horrifyingly might have to happen eventually. I started to bargain with myself: *I'll have two kids, but I'll have them young and really close together so that I can get it over with and enjoy the rest of my life.* Then, later on: *I'll just have one, that way I can shorten the whole ordeal by a couple of years.* It had honestly never occurred to me that one of my options was to not go down that path at all.

The realisation that a childfree life was something that would suit me very much came when I was diagnosed with a slew of gynaecological issues. First polycystic ovarian syndrome (PCOS), then a septate uterus, then endometriosis and adenomyosis. At this point I was in the thick of my postgraduate midwife studies. So while none of the professionals I was seeing actually said anything about what this would mean for my fertility, I knew that not only getting pregnant, but staying pregnant would likely be difficult. What should have been devastating news instead left me feeling ... lighter? I guess this information was like a layer of armour. If people asked too many questions about being childfree, I had the big red bail-me-out-of-this-conversation reply of 'I'm infertile'.

Infertile. I find it such an ungainly word. But women's health is full of coarse, brutal language to describe our bodies. Incompetent cervix, habitual aborter and failure to progress are just a few of the terms that I want to see banished from obstetric discourse forever. Another one that makes my skin crawl: socially infertile. A term used to describe people who don't have a partner or who can't become pregnant because their partner was born without XY chromosomes.

I fall into the socially infertile category. After going through a break-up in my early twenties, I had to admit to the people around me that no one ought to be terribly surprised if I bring home someone who isn't a cis man. I mumbled this into a bowl of risotto during a visit back home. My mum said it was a shock, my dad disagreed and reckoned he'd known all along. I have the distinct advantage of living in the inner north of Melbourne, so my friends barely even batted an eyelid. One only paused to frown and say, 'You didn't know that already?'

I did not know that already. My mid-twenties were spent wishing I had known a lot of things already. I wish I had known I was queer, I wish I had known that cheap wine invariably leaves you with a punishing hangover, and most of all I wish I had known what a midwife was when I left school. Instead I became a registered nurse. I fell into a job in a GP clinic, where the world of reproductive health was brought to my attention. I met people who had just found out they were pregnant, I saw them when they needed their whooping cough immunisations, and I hugged them when they came in for their postpartum check-ups. They brought with them the baby that had once been a second line on a pregnancy test and was now before me, pink and squirming. It amazed me. It still amazes me.

Some people find it a weird paradox: the childfree midwife. It's true, I don't want what they are experiencing. But consider this: you wouldn't think less of the oncologist that hasn't had cancer. To be a midwife is to be with the birthing person. In my role I see people for about twenty-five weeks of their pregnancy. I sit with them through the hours, sometimes days, of labour. And then, in contrast, once their baby is born, just a handful of home visits. Largely it's not my colleagues, or people who have had children, who find the childfree-midwife thing jarring. It's the people who are yet to have their baby, or don't know what a midwife is, who look at me like I have three heads when I tell them no, I do not have children, and no, I will not be having any. Some might think my choice is selfish. But I don't think any of the people who have had their baby with me would use that word to describe me. I get to give them so much more of myself. And to mirror parenting, when I give more, I get more in return. I treasure my job, being there to see someone bring their baby into this world is such a shiny honour that no matter how many times I see it, it never feels less bright.

So now, twenty-five years on from that playground conversation, I find myself unmarried. And childfree. I have a robust and fulfilling life. I have a partner who is a trans man. I adore him, he adores me and we both adore our childfree lives. We pour ourselves into our niblings, and when I read books to them that mention anything other than the gender binary and expected societal norms, it puts a lump in my throat and I feel jealous that this was not also my experience. For anyone considering a childfree life, or who have found themselves in this position unwillingly, know that it's not one marked by deprivation. For those of you with childfree friends or family, know that while having kids might not be for them, they still love yours more than you know.

Grace Hooper, midwife

Motherhood is full of wonder and sacrifice. It changes the course of our lives and our careers and our relationships, and it brings joy and pain. And we make room for all of this if it is the path we have chosen. But the choice to become a mother must also include the choice to not become one – a choice that should be universally protected for all women.

In June 2022, *Roe v Wade* – the landmark 1973 United States Supreme Court decision that gave women in the USA the right to an abortion for any reason – was overturned with devastating consequences for millions of women. In the USA and around the world, we asked ourselves: how could we have found ourselves here? It feels like a dystopian nightmare. A live episode of *The Handmaid's Tale*. A horror show. In a country that has no universal healthcare, no paid family leave and the highest maternal mortality rate of any industrialised nation with huge racial disparities within that statistic (black women are four to five times more likely to die from pregnancy-related causes than white women), the highest court in the land decided to no longer protect a woman's right to choose what's best for her body and her life.

This patriarchal abuse of power goes beyond abortion and further into the reproductive and women's health space. We live with language that drips with misogyny: miscarriage, incompetent cervix, inhospitable womb, trial of labour, geriatric pregnancy, failure to progress, socially infertile. We are gaslit into believing pelvic pain is normal and all part of being a woman. We don't talk enough about female pleasure, and many of us have grown up not understanding how our menstrual cycle works or even knowing what a vulva is. We feel socially induced shame and judgement for every decision and every turn our reproductive lives take – when we terminate a pregnancy or we can't conceive or we don't birth the way we'd hoped or we can't or choose not to breastfeed. And in many industrialised nations, Australia and the United States included, we are controlled through our pregnancies and births by a medical system that is not woman-centred but at the whim of policies and practices that ignore our emotional safety in favour of retaining patriarchal power and hierarchy, and then we come out the other side often traumatised and with very little, if any, postpartum care, and we're expected to be able to mother after all of that?

If we looked at the research and the evidence and took into account what's best for women's physical, emotional and mental health when it comes to conception, pregnancy and birth, we'd have free midwife-led continuity of care for all, resulting in far less trauma and happier, healthier families.

But here we are. The patriarchy reigns. And while nothing good can come out of the overturning of *Roe v Wade*, the tiny silver lining is that more people are angry and ready to fight. We can't and won't stand for it any longer. Every woman should be able to choose motherhood if and when it feels right to her – and be supported and cared for and respected on her journey, whatever turn it takes.

CORINNE'S STORY

No one ever imagines their motherhood journey will begin with loss, much less one that is 'chosen'. I fell pregnant when I was twenty-three, in the middle of a six-month-long trip with my now husband. I had been on the pill for years, yet somehow, in a hotel bathroom hours before boarding a flight to Rome, I saw my first two lines appear on a test. I was overjoyed, completely and utterly moved by the idea of life growing inside of me. But joy very quickly turned to terror, because sitting on the bed just outside the bathroom was the love of my life, my best friend for almost half my life, the man I knew would one day be the father to my babies, and a man I knew would be paralysed by fear at the idea of starting a family so young. Our stories around children were vastly different – I had seen my parents raise seven babies with ease, an experience of parenthood imbued with magic and safety and so much love (they were the reason I knew I always wanted to be a mama). But what Jake had seen, and what society had often reflected back at him, was very different. We were faced with an impossible decision, on the other side of the world to everything that felt safe and comfortable. The fact was, I wanted this baby with my entire being, and he was simply not ready.

There were only a few days between finding out I was pregnant and the pregnancy ending – we found out at five weeks, before our baby ever had a heartbeat, and I wanted it to stay that way. But the speed of it meant that before I had even given myself the opportunity to fully come to terms with the pregnancy, or had the opportunity to entirely understand the process of what my body was about to go through, I was already in a hospital in London, bleeding and in pain, as my body birthed for the first time.

The days and weeks that followed are still impossible to describe. I felt I was watching it from a distance. I was completely broken and numb, I was mourning a life and a future that ceased to exist anywhere outside of my mind. I cycled through a depth of emotions I had never imagined a human could feel, and I felt it all at once. I was angry, furious with Jake, with myself and anyone else who played a part in what had unfolded. I quickly became the villain in my own story, as did Jake, and it tested our relationship in unimaginable ways – there were moments I wanted him close, and others where I couldn't bear being near him. We were both in uncharted territory, a young couple trying to work our way through something society has deemed as wrong.

It was a loss I didn't know how to grieve – there's no handbook on how to do it. I had lost loved ones before and understood how to walk through that pain, but this was different. It's something women are expected to deal with behind closed doors, to not discuss openly for fear of offending others who believe they should have a say in what we choose to do with our bodies, or the decisions we make for our families.

Five years later, now a mama to two beautiful girls, I write this as I am about to enter the third trimester of growing our third magical being. There are still moments when the sadness will stop me in my tracks, where it will completely take my breath away, but I have learnt, and continue to learn, to be okay with it. These two little humans and their dada have brought me more joy, ease, utter contentment and love than I imagined possible, so I truly have no regrets, because for every moment of deep sadness there have been a thousand more extraordinarily magical ones.

It's taken me time to feel at peace with what happened, to no longer feel resistant to grieving the loss. I choose to not refer to what happened as an abortion or termination – it feels too medicalised, too heavy with judgement and void of emotion – but rather an early birth, one shrouded in sadness and heaviness, but a birth none the less. Because all pregnancies, one way or another, will end in a birth, and each birth will offer the mother an opportunity to grow and to learn, and to be presented with an entirely new reality to navigate.

While I don't regret where our story has taken us, I wish I had given myself permission to fully feel the pain, the insurmountable weight of it all – we may have made the choice to end our first pregnancy, but I refuse to believe that removes our ability to grieve it. I wish I had learnt to let go of other people's opinions sooner, to have remembered that we are not defined by a moment or a choice, and that while motherhood will crack your heart open in the most extraordinary ways, it may also bring moments of deep sadness. That there is no correct way to live, to start a family, to be a parent – no one-size-fits-all approach to this extraordinary gift of human experience that we are given – it is nuanced and beautiful, sometimes filled with uncertainty where it feels as though there is only darkness. But even in those moments there will always be some remnant of light, of goodness and of magic – it may just take a little bit longer to find it.

Corinne Milgrom-Marabel, mother of Naiya, Mahlia and Taj

Longing and loss

Choosing to have a child is the greatest leap of faith that exists in this life. There is no way of knowing just how long or short the path to parenthood will be, or if there will be a child at the end of it, or if that child will walk alongside us until our own deaths, as it should be. Heartbreak and loss and the unexpected can meet us at any point along the way.

The moment we start longing for a child is the moment we start planning our lives with them, almost as if there is no other option than for them to be born and to be by our side forever. But we cannot write about birth and life without also writing about loss and death. And while we may fear it, it is ever present in the lives of so many mothers.

I often find when I speak to women about their experiences of motherhood, they can be quick to dismiss what they have gone through, comparing it to the experiences of others and not giving themselves permission to grieve. Loss within motherhood can take so many forms and all experiences deserve to be acknowledged. Statistically, loss is devastatingly prevalent in the pregnancy and birth space – one in four will miscarry, one in four will terminate, six babies are stillborn every day in Australia – and it is so important we hear the stories of these women, and to also acknowledge that not all losses are recorded, like the loss of a dream for women who can't conceive.

In the stories that follow, Kate, Pippa, Heba, Mia, Natasha and Kristy-Lea share how the experience of loss has shaped their motherhood journeys. I am thankful to each of them for trusting me to share their stories.

To all mothers who have lost babies and children and who have experienced this raw and complex grief, I see you.

KATE'S STORY

Once upon a time, there was a woman who stood up, and cleared her throat. For there was a place inside her that both tripped her voice up and demanded she speak. Something that had her talk through the colour sepia.

Sepia is made up of three colours: burnt umber, olive green and black. It is hard to distinguish each when they are mixed on a palette. And even harder when they are used as a filter to make the images of one's life look antique: muddy and faded.

Sepia has been both the shade of our protagonist's misfortune and the hue of her ascendance. But then, it is always a choice as to what colour we gift our experiences; and why, she says, can't there be more than one?

Since she can remember, she always wanted children. In her youth, she would experiment with names, playing out the syllables to see if they sung:

A-n-o-u-k-T-a-y-l-o-r-J-o-n-e-s. S-o-p-h-i-a-Jo-n-e-s. A-r-c-h-e-r-J-o-n-e-s.

The men she dated all said they had never wanted children but, having met her, could see a burgeoning life they wanted to invest in. When that needed to become a reality, however, like most heroes facing the ultimate test, a mirror, they ran screaming.

Though he was part of making her childhood cot, her own father had run screaming when she was eleven years old. She hasn't seen him since. The pattern is a little too obvious, don't you think? But that's another story.

And so, the girl voted most likely to marry and make babies became an archetype no one had introduced her to as a kid. No one had read her stories of the cool aunt, or the woman who had an incredible career and travelled across the globe. Well, maybe some of the movies she watched in the eighties featured some savvy working girls, but they always had to end up with a Harrison Ford too. It wasn't enough for a woman to stand alone in her own power.

So, stand she did when she tried for a child on her own. Her mother had raised herself and her brother from the ages of four and two respectively. If she could do it ...

What she couldn't do as a single woman was try more than two times. For financial reasons, the expense of the IVF system on her own was an almost impossibility. And she wasn't prepared to bear a child severely in the red: that is, borrow from her superannuation as so many women are guided to do.

Aren't we supposed to affix the oxygen mask to ourselves first? What good does it do for mother and child if we sell it off?

This was not the first time she was a laudable mother.

Of course, she was never alone when she was trying for a child. She created a family long before her babies were seeded. At the time she needed to choose a sperm donor, she had five of her closest women friends come and read their letters (the reasons why they wanted to donate sperm) to help her choose a suitable papa. They ate cake and sipped chai and marvelled at the generosity of these unknown humans. She remembers rubbing the fertile ground between her belly button and pubes and saying, 'Look at all your amazing aunties. They are here for you.'

Burnt umber was the colour of these women, the colour of family and friends ... the colour of her boss who bowed their head at the time of her first miscarriage. Miscarriage is burnt umber. Rich in the knowledge that it is a miracle any one of us is here.

When she awoke at the hospital, seeping red, crows were outside her window. Later, at work, chirping erupted from a nest staff had all been watching. The chicks had been born.

Life or death is, indeed, anyone's guess.

The nest was housed in a tree with olive green leaves. Green. A colour so wealthy in metaphor our heroine had no choice but to fade. No choice but to grow from muddied browns and bow to the breeze and feed the air with oxygen and seed the earth with more life. To become a mother ... in most unexpected ways.

At almost forty-two she is invited to facilitate an initiative to bring joy to children through drama all over her state of Victoria. That year, she worked with 7000 children.

In the same year, she is invited to mentor burgeoning teachers for a most prominent university, to be on a board that ensures more children have access to theatre in Australia, and to speak in Iceland at a world congress about her work over the last two decades with young people.

It is here that she stands on a glacier to record a message for her nieces so they can see there are more colours to choose from. That there are other paths they can take.

And so, we end on a black canvas. The last shade needed to make sepia. Because she didn't have children of her own. Because all this was unforeseen. And confounding. And disorienting.

But it is also good. More than good because a black canvas welcomes stars, glittering, even in death.

Kate Ellis, drama coach, writer, community arts program developer and teacher

PIPPA'S STORY

I never thought much about motherhood as a young adult. Looking back I think I absorbed a narrative that it was 'selfish' to have only one child. My mum had told me that she found childbirth easier than periods. I guess I'd always assumed that I'd have a couple of kids without any trouble.

When we were in our late twenties my husband and I decided to stop using contraception. We had no reason to believe that we would have trouble conceiving, but after a couple of years I had some tests done. I received reports full of words that I didn't understand and found it very difficult to get straight answers. Doctors kept saying there was no obvious reason we weren't conceiving.

By the time I was thirty-five, I'd had a few pregnancies end in early miscarriage. I had made huge changes to my lifestyle and diet and was having regular acupuncture. I still wasn't getting (or rather, staying) pregnant, so we chose to do IVF. Round one resulted in five embryos and the first transfer was successful.

At twenty-one weeks, I went home for a rest between meetings. I was getting ready to go back to work when my waters broke. In shock, I drove myself to the hospital, where I was told the baby was still alive but wouldn't survive. The following morning there was no longer a heartbeat and labour was induced. I gave birth to a tiny, perfect, dead baby girl.

My grief was enormous, but the clock was ticking loudly and the pressure from the IVF clinic was intense. I had two unsuccessful transfers before I put my foot down. I needed more time to recover physically and emotionally.

After a break, embryo number four resulted in an anxiously monitored pregnancy. I had weekly check-ups in the high-risk pregnancy clinic, and eventually gave birth to a healthy baby girl. It was ten years since we'd decided to throw away the condoms and see what happened.

Our daughter was two when we decided to have one last shot at giving her a sibling. I was delighted when the transfer of our fifth embryo was successful. I was back to attending the high-risk pregnancy clinic each week, but felt healthy and positive. Then at a routine check-up, there was no heartbeat. It was absolutely devastating to realise this was happening again. Another induced labour, another beautiful, dead baby girl.

My twelve-year fertility journey resulted in seven pregnancies, two stillbirths and one healthy miracle child. Throughout that time, I often felt as if my life was on hold. I grieved missed opportunities, actual deaths and a life I didn't get to have. My daughter knows she has two sisters that didn't live, and that I am grateful for every moment with her.

Pippa James, mother to Ruby, Clover and Heidi

HEBA'S STORY

When my daughter was a year old she was diagnosed with stage 4 cancer. When you become a mother, you don't think you are going to outlive your child. When you become a mother, you have a vision of what you want your child's life to be. You have hopes and dreams and fantasies and you can see them growing up through the ages. But for me, motherhood is about making sure my child is surviving. Every day I think, could this day be her last? And no mother wants to think like that. For me, motherhood is everything I didn't expect but at the same time it is a type of love I can't explain. It is raw and deep and piercing, that love, and then having the knowledge that you could lose your child any day, it's suffocating.

Heba Shaheed, women's health physiotherapist and mother of Ruqaya

MIA'S STORY

Very early in my pregnancy I had a strong feeling that I would not be able to keep our baby safe. I had recurring nightmares that my son was stillborn. I didn't tell anybody, not even my husband.

My fears became so intense that I did whatever I could to avoid harm for my baby and in doing so developed obsessive compulsive disorder – particularly focused on hygiene and decontamination. Soon my hands were chapped and bleeding from washing and sanitising. I avoided meals prepared by anyone else. The compulsions didn't ease my fears, I had a deep sense that my baby was not safe and no extreme measure I took reassured me otherwise.

At our thirty-two week scan, I was nervous. The sonographer focused on the baby's brain. She left the room and brought back the obstetric sonologist. I asked him what he was seeing. He told me to be quiet and lie still so he could concentrate. I knew something was wrong.

More investigations over the next few days revealed that I was pregnant with a baby boy who had trisomy 18, a lethal condition that occurs at conception. Our baby Charlie was stillborn on a rainy Friday at 3.05 pm on his dad's birthday. I was quiet through his birth, my body numbed by the epidural and my heart broken knowing that he was not alive.

My inner knowing told me something was wrong and I had gone to extreme lengths to protect him but, unfortunately, nothing I did would have saved my baby boy.

Mia Elliott, consultant and leadership coach and mother of Charlie, Harry and James

NATASHA'S STORY

I remember people asking me what I wanted to do when I moved interstate to be with my now husband five years ago. I want to be a mum, I said. Many years later I am still yearning to hold that baby in my arms.

I found out I was pregnant for the first time in October 2021, three weeks before our wedding. Our five week and eight week ultrasounds went smoothly, our baby's little fluttering heartbeat was strong. We were so excited to see them again at our eleven week appointment, anxious and nervous to hear their heartbeat and see more detailed little features. Instead we heard, 'This doesn't look good. I'm sorry, your pregnancy is no longer viable.' I fell apart.

I chose to have a D and C and felt right about this decision. But as I was wheeled in I was overcome with sadness, knowing my baby would no longer be with me. In the days that followed I went looking for answers as to why my body had failed me. I took months off work and the ocean became my place for healing, walking in the shallows until I was able to immerse myself in the saltiness.

In among the fear, sadness, growth, strength and self-discovery, I never imagined becoming a mother would be so hard.

We had our first appointment with an IVF specialist a few weeks ago. And here I wait, hopeful.

Natasha Priolo

KRISTY-LEA'S STORY

I believe motherhood starts the moment you choose to be a mother. It's interesting that when you are pregnant for the first time and it's Mother's Day, it's not really celebrated as your first Mother's Day. It's only once the baby is here that you are seen as a mother. Normally I wouldn't think about that, but losing a baby changes how you see things.

For me, the choice to become a mother came about seven years into our marriage. When we got married, kids were on the agenda, but it took us a while before we were ready. We asked ourselves big questions in the lead-up like, *Why are we choosing this path? What will our parenting journey look like? Are we ready for this?* We thought that maybe we wouldn't have children – that if it wasn't a hell yes, then it was a no. In the end, I sent my husband, James, an email sharing what had been coming up for me, a desire I couldn't shake. It turned out he was feeling the same and we were ready to take the next step.

Parker's conception was very conscious. We did lots of preconception prep and fell pregnant on the first cycle. My whole pregnancy was intuition-led, very connected and so beautiful. I consciously chose to opt out of scans and chose an independent midwife and homebirth.

I waited patiently for labour to begin on its own and it did, at forty-two weeks and one day. I had twelve to fourteen hours of early labour, with things stopping and starting. I tried to see it as a normal day, but there was so much emotion. We were so excited to meet him. In the early hours of the second day, things felt different. I had been so connected to him every single day of this pregnancy and now I couldn't feel his movements as strongly, which immediately raised red flags for me. It was always part of our plan to go to hospital if something was wrong – you just never think you're going to need to.

We went to hospital for monitoring. They had a hard time finding his heartbeat with the doppler and an ultrasound confirmed it: Parker's heart had stopped.

Going back to that moment is utterly heartbreaking. We went from the peak of excitement to the depths of pain instantly. I went into shock, trying to process the impossible while still having contractions in a hospital room that was foreign to me. Thankfully, the midwives were incredible. There was not an ounce of judgement about our choices and they cared for us deeply.

They took us to a bereavement room in the birthing suite, which was completely separate from the rest of the maternity ward. I remember thinking, 'What happens now? Do I have a caesarean?' I didn't know what the process was when a baby dies. A bereavement midwife talked us through our options and recommended a vaginal birth because it would help my postpartum recovery, and any future births. They gave me space to labour, but my contractions had slowed down completely. I knew there was no way I'd be able to create an environment that was conducive to labour progressing, so I chose syntocinon and an epidural. Unfortunately, I had two failed epidurals. On the third attempt, it worked. We presented to the hospital at 8.30 am, the syntocinon started at 8.30 pm and my epidural finally worked at 4.30 am the next morning. I got some sleep and by 8 am, I was ready to push.

My son, Parker James, was born at 8.36 am on Friday 5 November 2021.

My sister was present for his birth and recorded it, and I am so happy she did because as much as it breaks my heart to remember that moment, it was so very special. There was so much fear before he was born, about what he might look like. But apart from his eyes being closed, he looked like a perfect little baby. I held him close. He was very long – 55.5 cm! He had the cutest little ears and nose just like mine, and he had my husband's bum chin and tiny curls in his hair. He was so beautiful.

That night, we slept with him in bed cuddled up between us. We had the option of taking him home or staying with him longer if we used the Cuddle Cot to keep him cool, but we chose quality over quantity. By Saturday night, we were home.

Sharing his story is how I mother Parker now. With grief, there is a lot of teaching that needs to happen. People often don't know how to communicate with you. I have learnt to ask for what I need and to be clear about how people can support me, which I think is valuable learning for any motherhood journey.

I feel him with me in different ways every day. He is woven into our every moment, and we have learnt to speak of him from a place of love, not just of pain.

I feel lucky to have always been seen and acknowledged as a mother in our circle. It is so important to honour a mother from the moment they decide to become a mother. Because that means their baby existed. Parker existed. And although he doesn't get to be here, we held him and we loved him for his entire life, and I will carry him in my heart for the entirety of mine.

Kristy-Lea Brown, mother of Parker

Pregnancy
and birth

As a doula and birth worker, this is a chapter close
to my heart.

I have witnessed time and time again how a supported, empowered
pregnancy and birth journey brings peace and positivity to the motherhood
experience and provides a source of strength and power when a mother
needs it most. As I wrote in my first book *The Birth Space*, a positive birth
is not necessarily how your birth unfolds – at home in a birth pool, with an
epidural in a hospital bed or surrounded by surgeons – but how respected
and cared for you felt throughout.

In this chapter, I share my three pregnancy and birth journeys alongside
insights from revered women working in this space. If you are on the cusp of
parenthood or are planning more children, I hope the words in this chapter
guide you to seek care that honours you, your body and your choices. If you
are finished this season of your life, I hope these insights help validate your
experiences and guide you to seek support if you need it.

Women are socialised from birth to conform, to not be the experts of their body and to outsource expertise about what's happening to them. In pregnancy, the safety aspect is deeply embedded. All we can do as care providers is make sure our interactions are reinforcing that women are the experts and constantly sending the message that you always have a choice.

"

Dr Rachel Reed
Midwife, author, educator, speaker, researcher,
consultant and mother of two

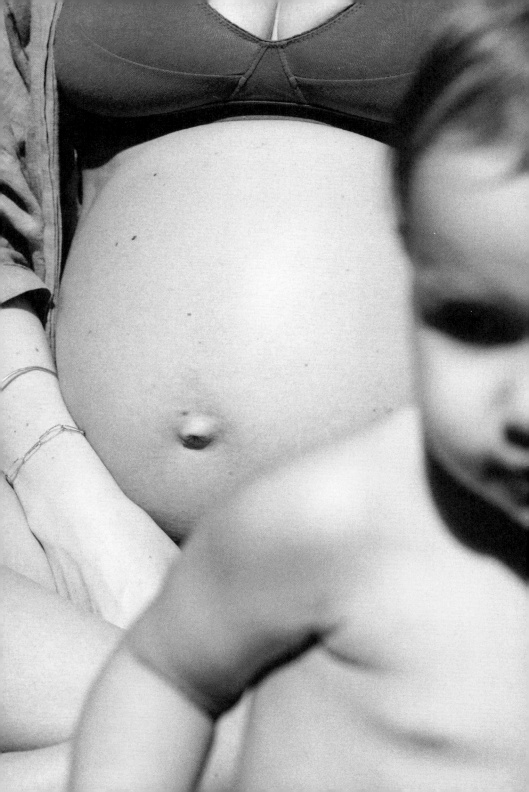

YANIKA'S STORY

I had the usual excited anticipation of being pregnant: to have beautiful photos, plan a baby shower, wear a bodycon dress (haha) and enjoy the supposedly most beautiful time in my life.

Instead, I had the opposite experience, suffering from hyperemesis gravidarum (HG) from six weeks in both my pregnancies, although I wasn't diagnosed until week fifteen in my first pregnancy because no one believed my symptoms were as severe as they were. I was told it was 'just morning sickness' but I knew it wasn't normal. It wasn't until I fainted at the doctor's after forty-eight hours of vomiting that I was finally taken seriously.

The cruellest part was that I kept thinking it would end each week. It didn't. I vomited uncontrollably until the night before I went into labour at thirty-eight weeks and four days – I had planned a hospital birth but she came quickly at home. Once my placenta was birthed it felt like a cloud had been lifted – my midwife said that my colour immediately returned to my skin. It was only then that I was able to process just how bad it had been.

The mourning came in my postpartum. When I looked back on my pregnancy, I was also looking ahead to future pregnancies because the chances of having HG again were high (80 per cent). When I did become pregnant again, I was hit even harder and it was then that the loss really dawned on me – I would never experience a 'normal' pregnancy or what 'normal' looked like in my dreams. I hate being pregnant and it's so sad to me that I've lost that experience because of this illness.

The only thing that kept me going in my second pregnancy was knowing it would probably continue to the end – I didn't have my hopes up like I did during my first pregnancy. I leaned into rest and relied heavily on my partner to be the primary carer for myself and our daughter. I lost a year of being in my daughter's life and it upsets me to this day. Not being able to play, run, talk, cuddle, read and lie down with her really took its toll on me, but she was incredible and adapted quickly – she would bring me my drink bottle or Powerade when I was in the dark bathroom vomiting and would pat my back and say she loved me and 'It's okay mama'.

One day I will tell both my daughters about my pregnancies and how I grew them and how sick I was, because unfortunately it might also be their reality one day. It's a bridge I will cross a long time from now but one I think about often.

I don't feel 'done'. I would love to try for another baby but I am scared and I am not sure it is something I can put myself and my family through – a catch 22 of wanting to grow our family but also being terrified that it could kill me.

If you are an HG mama, please know that whatever you are feeling is valid. HG is real but it is not taken seriously – we need more education, more support and more funding and I will continue to advocate for you and I hope we find a cure but in the meantime, I hope that you feel seen and heard.

Yanika Flynn, owner of biglittlethings store and mother of Alia and Amara

I have a photo on my fridge that is one of my favourites. I am twenty-five weeks pregnant with Camille and standing on a snow-trodden path in Central Park. I remember it was so cold that day my toes were numb. My coat no longer zipped up, and I had it pulled to the side so you could see my growing bump.

I walk past the photo a thousand times a day. The other day I lingered in front of it a little longer, thinking about the choices I made throughout that pregnancy and how they have shaped the pregnancies and births of all three of our children. In truth, it took until my fourth pregnancy – our third child – to find maternity care that felt honouring to me, someone who listened and who I felt equal to, not below. Like everything in motherhood, pregnancy and birth are seasons in which you will grow, learn and maybe also make mistakes – as I did. And while I wish I'd known more about the birthing landscape to make different choices earlier, I have deep compassion for myself back then – I was doing the best I could with the information I had.

For my first birth, I chose a hospital birth with an obstetrician simply because it is what my friends and family had done before me. At around thirty-six weeks we hired a doula and her care was life-changing. Before I gave birth, she asked me questions I hadn't known to consider and she taught us the importance of advocacy. During birth, she believed in me. And in my first few weeks as a mother she helped me navigate this new and tender world.

Camille was born on Mother's Day in 2014. James and I spent early labour wandering around our neighbourhood. I remember thinking how wild it was that everyone was just going about their day when I was having a baby! It was sunny and warm – the perfect spring day after a long and bitter winter. I was in awe of my body and I wasn't afraid. I laboured for hours at home and arrived at the hospital around 6 pm. I had my waters broken for no medical reason that I was made aware of, and by 8.15 pm she was born. I pulled her up to me just as the sun was setting and I had never felt more powerful or more overwhelmed.

What followed is still hazy. We started breastfeeding, my placenta was born with assistance I didn't consent to, and I stayed on my back on the bed for a couple of hours before being wheeled upstairs to the postpartum ward.

The Motherhood Space

I hadn't showered and no one was checking my blood loss. Upstairs a nurse told me to urinate and when I did, blood poured out of me. I haemorrhaged close to two litres that night and am still haunted by what happened in those early morning hours that I have very little recollection of. When I went back to see my obstetrician at my six-week postpartum appointment she dismissed and downplayed my experience, almost as if it was a blip in an otherwise seamless birth. When I asked what might have caused it, she said, 'I have no idea. These things happen.'

When I became pregnant with our second daughter, Audrey, I again hired an obstetrician because now I carried significant trauma and was hoping to find someone who would get to know me and my story and do everything possible to prevent another haemorrhage. I didn't connect with the doctor I found and often felt dismissed by her in our prenatal appointments. At thirty-seven weeks I found myself lying on the floor of our bedroom in tears, my hands across my stomach telling James I didn't want this doctor at my birth and I didn't want to birth in a hospital again. It was a visceral response – everything in my body was telling me to find a new support team but I thought it was too late to change and so I didn't.

Audrey was born on a warm autumn evening in March 2017. I laboured mostly at home and it was magic. I felt so connected to her and could feel her calm spirit holding me through each wave. At the hospital I found my rhythm in the shower and remember thinking that the pain felt good and it wasn't too intense and I was maybe even enjoying it. Just as I was starting to push, my obstetrician – who'd already broken my waters to 'speed things up' even when things were going lightning fast on their own – told me I 'wasn't allowed to' birth my baby in the shower and that I had to get on the bed. I wanted to say no. Everything in me wanted to say no. I stayed in the shower through a few more mighty contractions and felt Audrey move further down as my obstetrician hovered over me, getting impatient. So, like so many birthing women before me, I did as I was told and got onto the bed. Audrey was born into my arms thirty minutes later, pink, squishy and beautiful, but not on my terms.

This experience lit a fire in my belly and was one of the reasons I became a doula. I couldn't believe I'd been told to move from a position of comfort and ease into one in which I felt awkward and exposed – all for the doctor's benefit and the legacy of a patriarchal system that has been telling women to birth on their backs against all principles of physiology since the 1700s. For a long time I was angry at myself for not refusing her instruction, but I have since learnt and witnessed how hard it is to speak up when you are so deep in labour, let alone fight.

By the time I became pregnant with our third child, Freddie, I had been working as a doula for three years, attending homebirths and hospital births at private and public hospitals across Melbourne, and I knew exactly what care I would seek out: continuity of care with a midwife. I was one of the lucky few to be accepted into the midwife group practice program at my local public hospital, a model accessible to less than 10 per cent of birthing people in Australia, despite the fact that research shows it greatly improves outcomes for mothers and babies.

During my first appointment with my midwife at seventeen weeks pregnant, I finally felt seen and heard and cared for by a maternity care provider. The first thing she said to me was, 'Tell me your story.' And the tears came. No one had ever cared about my story before. I told her everything and she listened and she honoured and she validated me and my experiences and I finally felt safe.

I birthed Freddie at forty weeks and four days exactly the way I had hoped to: on my own terms without anyone telling me where to be or what to do. My midwife sat quietly in the corner, observing, holding space and honouring my wishes. I finally felt my waters break on their own, seconds before his head emerged, and with them released a sense of power and ecstasy that echoes through my mothering today. If only all women were given the love, care and opportunity to feel that.

I hear a lot of people saying that the maternity system is broken. It's not. It works perfectly. The system was set up to efficiently move a general population of women through it in the most cost-effective way with the minimum amount of variation because that is what it needs to function. It is not set up for women. It's failing women because it was never meant to not fail women. Induction falls into that. We need women's bodies to work like the machines that were conceptualised at the time of the development of maternity services as we know it, which came out of the industrialised era. Women's bodies were looked at as machines that needed to work more efficiently and of course medicine and technology could make them more efficient. That's how the system works and induction sits perfectly within it – we can't have variations of how long a woman is going to be waiting for her baby to come.

"

Dr Rachel Reed
Midwife, author, educator, speaker, researcher,
consultant and mother of two

Women are told, 'You can just say no.' But it is not a level playing field. You are at one of your most transformative but also most vulnerable moments in labour and you are being asked to make decisions that are coming across to you as life-and-death decisions. And not your life, your baby's life. You might have done all the work and have a wonderful plan for how you'd like to birth and then you go into the hospital and you say no to the first intervention suggested and you get the 'dead baby card'. Where do you go with that? How can you respond to that when you are in such a vulnerable position? How can your partner respond to that when they are putting the baby up against you? So 'no' doesn't come out, and there is not even a negotiation and then it starts the whole cascade of intervention and afterwards, the woman looks back and blames herself because she didn't say no, she didn't stand up for herself. I want to say to that woman and to all women, it's not your fault you didn't say no. How could you? How could you say no when there is a massive patriarchal hierarchy above you and you are at the bottom of the pile?

"

Dr Hazel Keedle
Midwife, author, researcher and mother of five

There is so much opportunity for empowerment in birth. But for the 97 per cent of women who birth in the hospital system in Australia (97.9 per cent in the UK and 98.4 per cent in the US) we are up against a system that tells us not to trust our bodies and deems us failures if our labours don't progress or if our inductions don't work. And then we blame ourselves and begin motherhood in a cycle of guilt and regret.

A recent Australian study called The Birth Experience Survey – a joint venture between Western Sydney University and the Birth Time Movement – explored the impact of care on women's birthing experiences. One of the questions they asked the 12,000 birthing people who participated was 'What would you do differently if you were to birth again?' The biggest overall comments? *Next time I'll get it right. I'll seek more knowledge. I'll get more support.*[1] They blamed themselves. They carried the guilt. And that is the saddest thing.

If you have ever felt this, please know you are not a failure. It was not your body that failed. It was the system that failed you. I know it is difficult to trust our bodies when we have been taught from a young age not to, and every little detail has been broken down and judged. But it feels like the ultimate reclamation of power and the patriarchy's worst nightmare for us to realise we have everything within ourselves to birth our babies in a way that honours our mind, body and soul – whatever that looks like to you.

When pregnant and planning for birth, seek care that is deeply honouring and respectful of your choices and your wishes. If you're hoping for a vaginal birth or a vaginal birth after caesarean (VBAC), hire a midwife and think about homebirth. If you are planning a caesarean, look into maternal-assisted and gentle caesarean births. Wherever you are birthing, learn about informed consent and the difference between hospital policy and your legal and human rights – which are two very different things. If you have the financial means, hire a doula to help you navigate the system and provide education and emotional support, and invest in bodywork to soften and release areas of tension, particularly around your pelvic floor. The more knowledge and support you have, the more positive your birth experience will be and a positive, empowered birth will set you up beautifully for postpartum and your motherhood experience.

Knowledge is power. Equip yourself with the tools. Birth on your terms.

[1] Information obtained during an interview with Dr Hazel Keddle.

The negative effect of the patriarchy on mothers and birthing people starts at menarche through menstrual shame and is woven through our fear-based medical system that seeks to control the birth process. This misogyny and oppression of women increases fear, pain, intervention and birth trauma. We must prepare for birth by becoming informed and making informed decisions. Step into self-authority and sovereignty and decline what you know is not right for you. Listen to your inner knowing and don't get talked out of it.

"

Jane Hardwicke Collings
Women's mysteries teacher, shamanic craftswoman,
midwife, writer, teacher, mother and grandmother

MONIQUE'S STORY

I'm currently thirty-four weeks pregnant and when I think about becoming a mother, the tears come. I'm so emotional these days and I fear I haven't really had a chance to stop and think about how I'm actually feeling and about what's to come. The truth is, I'm feeling everything at once. I'm so excited to hold my little one in my arms, but I'm scared that I'm not as prepared as I should be. Will I know what to do? Am I running out of time to learn everything I wanted to before our baby arrives? Time is moving so fast.

After a tough start with morning sickness, I'm now loving every minute of being pregnant. I look forward to the days we'll take our little one on beach walks and around our neighbourhood, and I can't wait for the play dates they'll have with their cousins. But I also know that everything in our lives is about to change and I'm not sure I am prepared for that. Am I as prepared as I can be for birth and raising our child? I'm not sure you can ever be. With millions of thoughts running through my head, and hundreds of things I still need to do, what I do know for sure is that I'm lucky to be surrounded by the most supportive friends and family and so many amazing mothers that I look up to and learn from each day. Most of all, my mother. And knowing my beautiful sister will also be by my side during birth puts me at ease. I'm confident everyone close to me will help guide me every step of the way. Not to mention my incredible fiancé, who is the most excited of all. We may not be fully ready, but we'll ride the waves of this adventure together and I wouldn't want it any other way.

Monique Zender, publicist and mother of Delilah

Maybe it didn't go to plan. Maybe you are like the millions of women who happen to go 'overdue' – up to forty-two weeks is seen as normal but not treated as normal – and so you are induced and then you get all the interventions and then you're told you were a failure to induce and you didn't dilate and so you had a caesarean and you feel guilt, like it was just another thing your body wasn't good at. That is not an easy experience to heal from physically or mentally. We internalise the language and we absorb the guilt, and then we're expected to be perfect mothers? How? How are you meant to gain back your control in a society where you are told you are never good enough? Please know that it was not you, that you were part of a system and that system set you up to fail.

"

Dr Hazel Keedle
Midwife, author, researcher and mother of five

Women are told, don't have a homebirth for your first baby. My opinion? For God's sake, get this experience for your first baby because then you have that power and you do not have to fight to get it back. The ideal situation – whether it be at home or hospital – is for you to be engulfed in the care of a midwife who is going to tell you how amazing you are constantly. To have that person beside you who really believes in you and believes in the strength and power of women. Then you go into your birth with this incredible support team around you – and the more support the better, get your doula on board, get your partner trained up – a team of people who are knowledgeable and excited about birth and who believe in you and will help you navigate whatever comes up.

"

Dr Hazel Keedle
Midwife, author, researcher and mother of five

Birth trauma

It is estimated that one-third of all mothers worldwide experience birth trauma, which can be physical or emotional harm leading to devastating short- and long-term consequences for women and their families.

The World Health Organization recognises that abuse in childbirth is a violation of fundamental human rights, yet in most countries – Australia, the US and the UK included – there is no legislation against causing psychological harm to women during pregnancy and birth, such as disrespectful care or obstetric violence.[2] There is, however, the risk that a care provider will lose their registration if they do physical harm. They are impacted by their policies, by their guidelines, by their colleagues, by their registrations and by their fear of losing their job. That fear can lead to coercion, bullying, and deep psychological harm for the mother, which can manifest in her blaming herself and her body for a birth that didn't go as she had hoped and this experience echoes into her motherhood journey and for generations to come.

Birth trauma can happen in any birth setting: at hospital, in the home, under obstetric or midwife care, during a physiological birth or a caesarean birth or an epidural birth.

I have witnessed it many times, and families I have supported have been given the 'dead baby card' – told that if they decline the induction or other interventions then their baby might die and that the death will be their fault. What is a couple supposed to do with that information? They can try to push back, ask for the risks associated with the induction or intervention, information they have a legal right to, but then they are often not given the full picture and deemed uncooperative and feel as if their choices have been taken away from them. They've lost their power, they don't feel heard, they don't feel seen, and trauma sets in.

It's devastating and the consequences are far-reaching, often resulting in mothers absorbing guilt, having difficulties breastfeeding and bonding, potentially leading to PTSD, depression, anxiety, impacts on future births and a story the birthing woman will carry for life.

In the last decade, and following years of lobbying by women's rights groups, public health and professional organisations and researchers, Latin American countries including Brazil, Argentina, Venezuela and some Mexican states have enacted laws against obstetric violence and mistreatment of women during pregnancy, birth and postpartum.[3]

The only way we will ever see change in our systems is to follow suit and ensure care providers are at risk of losing their licence and also face potential criminalisation for psychological as well as physical harm. It's the very least women deserve, to know they will be given full autonomy in the birth space and protection against abusive, coercive, controlling behaviour by the people whose job it is to care for them.

[2] World Health Organization. *The prevention and elimination of disrespect and abuse during facility-based childbirth: WHO statement.* No. WHO/RHR/14.23. World Health Organization, 2014.

[3] Williams CR, Jerez C, Klein K, Correa M, Belizán JM, Cormick G. Obstetric violence: A Latin American legal response to mistreatment during childbirth. *BJOG: An International Journal of Obstetrics & Gynaecology.* 2018.

When women have a traumatic birth, right from the beginning, they feel bad about their mothering, whether they say it or not. And then when people say things like, 'Oh but your baby is healthy, let's move on', what they are doing is interrupting her energetic healing process. When I work with mums – and I used to also work with babies but I found when I worked with the mamas I didn't have to work so much with the babies – I work in alignment with the body to heal trauma. When a woman gives birth there is a physical and also an energetic portion to it: the womb dilates and the spirit door dilates and there is movement of that child's birth flow down the canal and onto the chest, and that can get interrupted at various points. So if a woman gets induced, for example, that energetic opening may never happen and she may feel like she didn't get something, but isn't sure what that something is. Or she may partially dilate and then fatigue sets in, or the baby is extracted or a caesarean is performed, and something feels incomplete for her in the birth flow. When women are in this energetic dilation they are very sensitive so they imprint deeply. So things that don't seem problematic to the providers or to the partner can be deeply problematic to the woman because she feels very open. What I want for every woman is to have a beautiful clear birth field where that flow is nice and strong so she can feel it and then also use it, because it can be medicine. We never want trauma but when you put healing to trauma you make the most potent medicine there is.

”

Tami Lynn Kent
Author of *Wild Creative, Wild Feminine* and *Mothering From Your Center*, and mother of three sons

Tending

The birth of your baby heralds a season of true vulnerability. This season of tending – to your needs and your baby's – is open and raw and beautiful and hard. This is a season that demands you to slow down, receive help, surrender and be witnessed. Very soon you will be the one holding your family together as you once did and will do again forever. Let yourself be held during this time and shut the outside world off for a while.

This is a season of rocking, shushing, feeding and holding around the clock. It is the season when quiet rage will creep in when you watch your partner walk out the door with ease and you feel trapped literally and figuratively – under a sleeping baby and in a life you don't recognise. This season brings with it the greatest transformation of your life – the transition from maiden to mother. It is so great you may at first resist it but you will transform nonetheless; there is no other way. It is a season in which even basic self-care seems to be a monumental task and you wonder, will it always be like this? Is this my life now? I am on the other side of this season so I can promise you it is not, but I also know how endless it feels and how dark the nights are.

This is a season rich with lessons, the greatest of which is trusting and knowing that you are enough.

When we give birth,
we don't just give birth
to our baby, we give
birth to the mother this
baby has come for.

"

Jane Hardwicke Collings
Women's mysteries teacher, shamanic craftswoman,
midwife, writer, teacher, mother and grandmother

The first forty days

I am in awe of new mothers. It is such a big time – the most radical of life shifts.

Hormones and emotions are all over the place. You are doing your absolute best. Taking it minute by minute. Finding your rhythm. But it's so hard. It's painful. There is endless doubt. It's exhausting beyond belief. Your body is raw and unrecognisable. You love your baby but pine for your old life. If you have older children, you miss them desperately and feel guilty you have such little time with them. And while you might on some level know these days are fleeting, when you are so deep in them, they truly feel never-ending.

In these first few days and weeks postpartum – a sacred period of time known as *the first forty days* – allow yourself to be held, prioritise rest, make space for your body to heal and time to connect with your baby, which doesn't always happen instantly. Many cultures around the world recognise the importance of this time of deep rest. In China it is known as sitting the month and is a strict set of rituals designed to restore a woman's life force. Throughout Latin America, women practice la cuarentena (literally, the quarantine) where female relatives move in to support the new mother. And in India, new mothers are fed a diet of warm, easy-to-digest meals and given daily warm oil massages to aid recovery.

In the west, we're not so good at protecting these tender first weeks. Mothers are overwhelmed with visitors sometimes hours after giving birth. We are gifted onesies and cute toys but rarely anything that honours our needs, like a postpartum doula or a nourishing meal or company from women who know how to hold space without imparting well-meaning but often unhelpful advice. Our culture does not recognise the importance of this time, but that doesn't mean you can't. Plan for and protect your first forty days so you have what you need to rest and feel supported. And then, as the weeks turn into months and the months turn into years, give yourself grace and continue to ask for help when you need it. Our needs as mothers might change but the need for support never leaves us. Postpartum is forever. We cannot do this alone.

It may seem like the world is going on without you but there is so much value in mothering. It is the most important role that exists in our world. We all need to be mothered. We all need care and love and a sense of belonging. Society may not value the ability to provide care to a vulnerable person, but try to cultivate that value yourself. Even when it is redundant, boring, and mundane, it is so important.

"

Kara Hoppe
Psychotherapist, author, teacher and
mother of Jude and Dion

Your immediate postpartum needs centre on nourishment, rest and emotional support. You are bleeding, you may have injuries and trauma from birth, you might be learning to breastfeed and experiencing afterpains every time you feed. Constipation and night sweats are common, so are sore bleeding nipples and engorgement.

Our hormones drop dramatically after birth and really mess with our emotions. You might be on an oxytocin high and then a couple of days later the tears come – and keep coming. You may not feel an instant connection to your baby and that is okay and normal. This kind of deep love can take weeks or even months to unfold and I wish we talked about this more.

For all of these reasons and a million more, you need to live these days in a safe, secure bubble. Say no to visitors and stay in bed. I know it's hard to slow down when we are conditioned to hustle, work and show how we are being productive. But I promise you, resting and feeding and healing and holding your baby all day *is* work. It is the world's most important work – the problem is, our culture doesn't recognise it as such and so we feel we must keep going and keep doing.

Plan for this period, know that it is normal to feel you should be doing 'more' and so when those feelings come up, remind yourself – or better still, have those around you remind you – that you are doing so much and that you need to give yourself space and time to physically heal and emotionally recalibrate to this new season. To allow this to happen, rally your village and bring in support. Only allow those people in who will show up for you and your family, who you can be vulnerable in front of, who you don't need to tidy up for, who will bring you food and run your errands and clean your house and wash your milk-stained clothes and run you a bath and hold your baby and hold your hand. This is the time to also invest in help if you are in a position to do so. Support for new mothers and families is an area woefully neglected by governments in too many nations – all mothers should be given free access to midwives, doulas, pelvic floor physiotherapists and lactation consultants and all parents should be given equal and extended paid parental leave – but it's not a reality for most, so do what you can to rally support so you have a soft place to land in these tender early days.

The Motherhood Space

As the weeks pass and you start to find your rhythm, think about what you need to sustain your days ongoing. What matters the most to you and helps to support your mental, physical and emotional health? For me it was making sure I showered every morning. In my early months postpartum, and still today, if I miss my shower my whole day is thrown off. When I recognised it as an essential need, to be able to close the door and have five minutes to myself under hot water, I told James and we shifted things to make it happen. What is your metaphorical shower? For some it's a cup of tea in bed, for others it's a walk on their own, for many mothers it's knowing their partner will be there through the night to support them. Even if you are breastfeeding, there is so much a partner can do at night to help – settling, changing nappies, being a source of comfort in the dark. If you're a partner reading this, never leave a new mother alone overnight. This is often the time she needs you most.

I wish someone I loved sat with me in the early days and said, 'Mama, what you are doing right now is important and deeply valued in the community. There is no need to justify your role as a mother to anyone. You are doing more than enough. Thank you.'

"

Kate Bloom
Birth and postpartum doula and
mother of Jozie, Pixie and Dusty

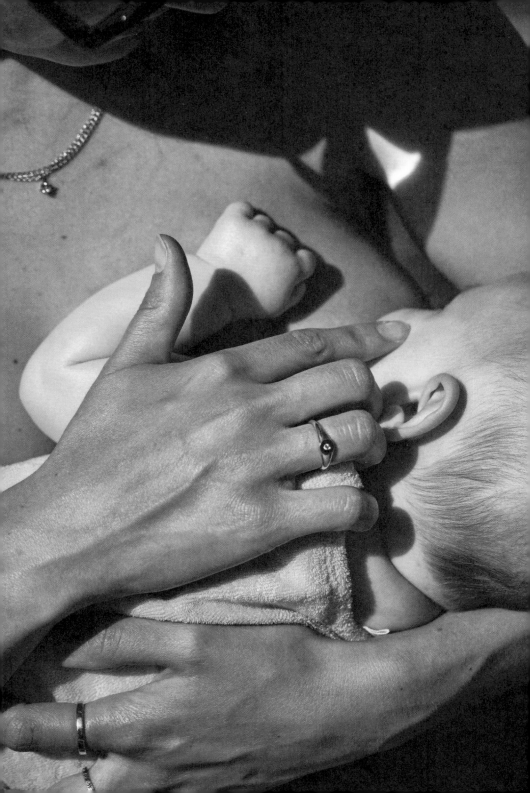

To all mothers I want to say, lying with your baby all day is doing something. You are doing so much. You are massively building the emotional foundation for their brain development and also for your own. I know it is hard because it is so invisible but the next time your partner comes home and asks what you did all day, tell them, 'We had a really intense day. We laughed, we cried, we slept, we fed and I am very slowly building the foundations of our baby's brain development, and also my own.' Co-regulating your baby is so physically and emotionally exhausting and it is such deep work and I don't think anybody outside of this intense mothering and parenting space understands how huge it really is.

"

Greer Kirshenbaum, PhD
Neuroscientist, doula, infant sleep specialist
and mother of one

ROWENA'S STORY

The moment I became a mother was not at all how I had imagined. Lying on a surgery table, glancing over at our baby on a resuscitation table. No initial embrace, no crying as she entered the world.

Similarly, the days and weeks that followed were not what I had prepared for. My early mothering days were spent sitting beside a humidicrib while my daughter recovered in the Special Care nursery. I wanted so desperately to cuddle her and feed her, but instead had to allow her to rest and gain strength, which was heartbreaking and went against every last shred of mothering instinct I had. I was left to sit by her and pump every three hours, day and night, to make sure my milk supply was not stunted, in the hope that I would one day be able to breastfeed her.

I was a shell of myself: recovering from a caesarean, bleeding, sore all over, emotionally and physically exhausted. And doubting myself in every aspect of motherhood. I felt that the medical staff were the experts and I was an onlooker. This was one of the most lonely experiences I have had to endure as a mother.

For ten days and nights my partner and I drove home with an empty car seat, to an empty bassinet and an eerily quiet house. Each morning we would wake early and return to the hospital. Sitting by her. Watching. Pumping. Waiting.

The day we were allowed to get her out for skin-to-skin was a triumph. That feeling of her skin on mine is something I will never forget. Warm. Sticky. Soothing. Fumbling with the leads and tubes attached to her became second nature to me.

Rolling with the daily highs and lows of having a sick baby, I came to realise there is never a linear journey to recovery when you are a parent of a baby in Special Care or NICU. It was a rocky journey out of there but we made it. Through much pain and practise we did eventually establish breastfeeding and I continued to feed her until she was fifteen months old. But in these early days I felt like a failure. There didn't seem to be any correlation between how hard I tried and the results I was getting, with feeding, sleeping and settling.

It took me a good six months to find my intuition and to build a loving connection with her – to really feel like she was mine. I think having all autonomy taken away from me during those early days of her life really impacted my mothering journey, and I doubted myself even with the smallest decisions.

Rowena Cooke, postpartum doula and mother to Sonny and Rua

The Motherhood Space

I wish all mothers knew that everything is a cycle and if you give yourself over to the cycle then it will change, but if you don't surrender to it, it will take so much longer to emerge from it. For example, the first six to twelve weeks of new parenthood might seem like a long time of not exercising, it might seem like a long time of staying close to home, it might all feel like a long time, but really in a lifetime it's such a short time. The gains that you get from respecting this period are invaluable and will stay with you for the rest of your life. What you gain can give you a lot of strength. We only hear stories of all the ways we become weakened and depressed postpartum, but we can actually come out of it so much stronger if we respect this sacred period.

"

Kimberly Ann Johnson
Author, somatic experiencing practitioner, sexological bodyworker, birth doula and mother of Cece

Pelvic care

Pelvic care is essential for all birthing people, regardless of how your baby was born. Your pelvis is put under enormous pressure as your uterus grows, which can lead to incontinence, prolapse and other common – but not normal – postpartum conditions.

It is recommended you see a pelvic floor physiotherapist during your pregnancy to help you prepare for birth and then again at around six weeks postpartum. If you can, seek out a physio who is trained in Tami Lynn Kent's Holistic Pelvic Care™. Tami has trained practitioners worldwide in her holistic approach to postpartum healing which combines energetic and intuitive body and breathwork to meet you where you are at, hear your story and support your journey.

Here, Tami shares her work in her own words:

'Holistic postpartum care for mothers is essential. It is why I created the bodywork that I do called Holistic Pelvic Care™. I was working as a women's health physiotherapist in the hospital and I was seeing lots of women later in life who had issues from childbirth that had never been addressed and that had accumulated. Their body had compensated so when they went through menopause and their hormones changed they had leakage and prolapses that were maybe asymptomatic or slightly symptomatic before. And I thought, why aren't we working on this sooner? Then I had a baby and felt the changes in my own body, the stretching and the shifting, and there was absolutely no care. In response, I created a bodywork practice that combines my women's health knowledge and working intuitively with the body, with an energetic component and a woman's breath and meditation component so she's part of the process.

My goal is to get more providers to understand this deeper level of work where we are reading and working with the body. We are in this dance with the pelvic bowl, really honouring the woman and supporting her in whatever way she needs. Some women have a traumatic birth and need medicine, some women have a pregnancy loss and need support, some women had really good mothering and they feel sturdy in that, some women had a really wounded mother and they are realising their wounds and also trying to give what wasn't given. It's a way of working energetically and space-holding that reads that woman's field and gives support to her. There is nothing like being nurtured when you are mothering. When you start caring for someone outside of your body there is so much to that process. We work on helping mothers come all the way through the experience and feel supported, feel loved and feel capable. Often how her birth experience went will set in motion in her mind, am I a good mother or a bad mother? We do a lot of healing around birth trauma to help set the woman into her own strength and into her own capacity.'

Maiden to mother

A little while ago, I received a middle-of-the-night text from a friend: 'Did you feel like a mother straight away? I don't know how I'm supposed to feel.'

She had just had her first baby and was standing where every mother has stood before her: deep in her transition, not able to go back but not sure how to move forwards. Untethered is the best word I can think of to describe the feeling. I felt it too, although not immediately.

It took me many months to realise that Camille's birth was also the birth of me as a mother, and that I had to shed and mourn my old self before I could fully step into this new identity and honour the rite of passage I was moving through.

I went straight back to my old life just days after Camille was born, a city life rich with gallery openings and rooftop parties and brunch and sample sales. Just as I had hoped, she fitted perfectly into our busy days and nights and somehow even slept well in our studio apartment. I went back to work full time when she was just four months old and pumped endless bottles of milk for her in my short breaks between meetings. We had a nanny and also my mum looking after her and I ran home every night so I wouldn't miss bathtime and stories. It wasn't the motherhood I had imagined and my heart broke every morning I had to leave her, all squishy cheeks and arms outstretched for me, but in a way it was also a relief. Being at work and in a job I had done for years was easy. I knew myself in that role and I was constantly rewarded and acknowledged. Motherhood felt as far from that as possible. There were no answers to the questions I was frantically searching Google for at 2 am. I felt out of my depth, overwhelmed and unsure. There was so much to learn and I was constantly looking outside of myself for reassurance, instead of listening to my gut and watching my baby.

Loving Camille was the easy part, she was and is an absolute joy, but everything else felt so foreign. So when it came time to go back to work, with my heart simultaneously breaking, I didn't resist. I knew she was being cared for and loved by our village and I needed more time to reconcile the hugeness of it all.

Women can honour and revere
their maiden (spring/birth), mother
(summer/childbirth), maga (autumn/
menopause) and crone (winter/
retirement) life seasons by living them
fully. To do that, we need to understand
them in the context of our lives and the
roles and responsibilities of each life
season. We need to understand, honour,
and celebrate our rites of passage that
create a new version of us as we shift
season. We need to stand in our power
and be who we are, not what we think
others want us to be.

"

Jane Hardwicke Collings
Women's mysteries teacher, shamanic craftswoman,
midwife, writer, teacher, mother and grandmother

A rite of passage is a transition that marks the end of one season and the beginning of another. For women, the most transformative are those of maiden to mother to maga to crone. When we transition from each of these seasons to the next, we need people to hold space for us so we can process what it all means, shed all that is no longer serving us and emerge anew. The problem so many mothers face today is that we are spiritually and often also geographically removed from the village of women we need to hold us through the biggest rite of passage there is – that of becoming a mother – and because the wisdom and the stories are not shared we can find ourselves fumbling in the dark wondering if we are the only ones who have felt like this.

I wish all mothers were honoured in their pregnancies and given the opportunity to sit down with the women they love to hear how they wrestled with the grief that came when they realised their old life was gone forever and this new one felt so different – when their relationships changed around them, their bodies softened and they felt so out of their depth in the early days and months and years of motherhood. I wish we were held by our friends and elders who have crossed this threshold before us. That when those people visit us in our tender postpartum days, they move past the baby and come and sit by us and ask us how we are feeling about it all. The birth of you as a mother is the greatest opportunity there is to come into your power but we cannot, and should not have to, do it alone.

I know for many of us it can feel woo-woo and uncomfortable to sit in a circle with other women and storytell, but I have come to learn that this is medicine we all need. We regularly hold mothers' circles at the women's space I created in Melbourne and I remember one gathering in particular where a pregnant woman joined us. She was the last in the circle to share and after hearing the stories of five mothers before her she simply said, 'Thank you. I feel I know a little more about a place that until now has felt so far away and foreign, so unknowable. I feel as if I've been let in.'

Of course, you do not have to sit physically in a circle of women to gather this wisdom. Reach out to your mum friends, start a text group, share the realities of what you are going through. Hopefully you will be met with understanding, support, guidance and people who listen when you need it most. Remember that you are never alone, no matter what you are going through.

I don't think we have enough conversations and frameworks around transitions and rites of passage. When our daughters move from childhood to womanhood, how are we honouring that? How are we showing them a pathway, getting around them as a circle of matriarchs and saying, here is what womanhood is, here are the stories we hand down, here is the sovereignty, here is how you know yourself outside of the culture that is telling you who you are? And how are we honouring women in their pregnancies, when they are on the precipice of completely transforming who they are? We need a framework that says, I see you, I know that you want this and this is joyous and also, there is pain and suffering in this as you reconcile and wrestle with who you have been and what you are leaving behind: the grief of the life that was or that might have been that is no longer. If we had a framework for her every step of the way we would have a very different understanding of what it is to live in a season of cycle and be a woman who centres her own empowerment and growth rather than relying on validation and value from a patriarchal structure.

,,

Julie Tenner
Intimacy and relationship coach, doula and
mother of Heath, Jade, Lola and Gwen

I finally accepted my transformation one night just after Camille turned one. She woke around 2 am and I breastfed her on the couch overlooking our fire escape. Her chubby hand rested gently on my breast as she fed and as I watched her, I knew I didn't want to resist it any longer. I was ready to move deeper into the fire. I wanted to be with her more and I was in the privileged position to make that happen.

The next morning I quit my job and we made plans to move home to Australia. The urge to leave the city and a job I had worked so hard for was strong. Many people said I was making a huge mistake – how could I walk away when things were going so well and I was reaching my career peak? The truth is, it didn't matter to me as much as it once had. My priorities had shifted. More than anything, I wanted to be with Camille more. I had missed her so much.

The loss of identity has been unexpected. I would say that I was abundantly ready for motherhood. I was ready to give up 'me' for her, but I also didn't actually know what giving up 'me' meant. It's not a bad thing, just something I couldn't have prepared for. Something I had to experience to understand.

"

Jessica Hart
Model and mother of Baby and Glorious

ELAINE'S STORY

I loved my life ... before I found out we were pregnant. I cried a thousand tears the day I did the test – tears of fear, doubt and anxiety.

I am an only child and while I had a wonderful upbringing, I was never really sure about kids – I'm ambitious and always striving for perfection and my happiness came from success and achievement in my creative and professional endeavours. And it was all going so well.

Luckily, I had a pretty good pregnancy. But the moment our baby was born, my mental health spiralled. The birth did not go to plan so I was recovering both mentally and physically from the trauma. Then the new parenthood snowball: lack of freedom and sleep, isolation, no family support, low milk supply, chronic nipple thrush, all in the midst of another COVID lockdown and living in a shoebox rental while finishing our renovation. I cried every day.

Some people say that having a baby gives a sense of purpose to their life. For me it was the opposite. Having a baby took away my sense of purpose, it put a dampener on all my dreams and ambitions and I was struggling to find a way out of the fog. Being the proactive person that I am, I needed to find a solution and that came in the form of a postnatal depression diagnosis, a referral to a psychologist and to Masada Hospital Early Parenting Centre (aka sleep school).

It felt like it has been seven and a half months of torture with a brief interlude of a couple of months where my mum came from overseas to help, which made all the difference. Then out of nowhere, she was diagnosed with stage 4 terminal cancer (that's a story for another day) and she had to move interstate.

Thank goodness for the amazing nurses at Masada Hospital, they saved me. Literally from night one, my baby went from waking five to seven times a night to sleeping through for twelve hours with two solid day naps. I finally felt like I could see the light of piecing together some semblance of my old life. I was starting to be approached about some interesting work projects and that felt exciting.

Then, out of nowhere, I felt a weird sensation deep in my belly. Fast forward two days and I'm sitting in the ultrasound chair being told I was more than nineteen weeks pregnant. WTF. I literally had no words! I had already sold all our newborn things because I told my husband that I was never going to go through that again. But, alas, it seems like the universe had other plans for us.

As I write this, I am twenty-five weeks pregnant and honestly still trying to process everything. I am terrified of going through the same experience with a fourteen-month-old in tow ... and the financial stress of being on a single income for an extended amount of time cannot be overlooked.

I am, however, trying to make a promise to myself. To not set myself expectations about what kind of birth I should have and not feel guilty that I am not the 'perfect' mother. To be kinder to myself and to acknowledge that I will probably be a happier mother if I integrate work back into my life. I have a new-found respect for all the women I see who are 'successfully' doing the juggle, and it's these people who give me hope that I can get back to loving my life once again.

Elaine Tiong, stylist and mother of Mila and Smith

Intuition

A newborn baby's instincts are strong.

If placed down low on their mother's belly, they will crawl towards the breast, latch on and start feeding without the need for help or guidance. This magic yet basic human instinct can take time, and will only happen if we are patient and give them space to find their way, resisting the urge to interrupt their flow with scales and swaddles and schedules and bright lights and other harsh realities of life in the world.

A newborn mother's instincts are also strong, yet we also have much in our way. Conditioning and cultural pressure. Expectations from family, friends, partners and ourselves. Judgement. Google. Instagram. Forums. Podcasts. Apps. Articles. Mothers' groups. Doctors who don't listen and put our concerns down to 'overreacting mother'.

We are often told to trust our intuition – but, seriously, how? We have never been taught to heed our gut or womb wisdom. From a young age, we have been conditioned to look outside of ourselves for answers: to be a good girl, to conform, to seek external reassurance. And then when we become mothers, the voices and the pressure become louder and the stakes become higher. How are we supposed to drown it all out and tune in to what we know to be true?

I think the first step is understanding the cultural context in which we are living and the messages – subtle and not-so-subtle – we are constantly receiving. For example, our instinct when we become pregnant might be to share the news immediately, but there is a societal expectation that we keep it quiet for twelve weeks, which also means so many of us suffer in silence if we miscarry. When our babies are born and we're cuddling them on the couch all day long, relatives visit and tell us to stop spoiling them and creating bad habits. We might want to breastfeed well into toddlerhood but we're not seeing that in our Instagram feed, so is it okay? I think our instincts are particularly strong when our children are sick, but there's also that voice in our head – often influenced by a partner or a doctor – telling us not to overreact. I have been sent home from the emergency department many times, only to come back hours later with an increasingly sick child. I've advocated and fought to have them admitted and have been right every time. We know what is right for our children, we know it deep in our bones, but the external messages are constant and loud and overwhelming and we are often caught in the middle, exhausted, trying to make sense of it all.

When my sister Justine was pregnant for the first time she had a feeling towards the end of her pregnancy that her baby needed more time to grow before they would be ready to join us earthside. As her due date passed and she crept towards forty-two weeks, she was encouraged to come into hospital every second day for monitoring, which she did. Her pregnancy was low risk, her baby's fluid levels and CTG readings were consistently good and despite there being no red flags, she felt immense pressure to induce. 'You know you're putting your baby at risk', was the constant message, without any evidence to back it up. She was being worn down by the system but her intuition was strong. She resisted and went into labour spontaneously at forty-two weeks and two days – almost unheard of in a hospital setting in Australia. Her baby girl Edie was born healthy, thriving and tipped the scales at just over three kilograms. She just needed a bit more time and her mother knew that. I am in awe of her for being that strong. I'm not sure I could have been.

Sometimes it is hard to listen in and trust what our bodies are telling us. And in those times I think it's really important to seek guidance from the people you trust, who you know won't bring judgement or their own stories to the conversation. As I have sunk deeper into motherhood and grown in confidence, it has become easier to block out the messages that once drowned me and realise there are no rules, that I can parent my way and only James and I know what is best for our children. And when things feel murky (which happens most days), I call my family or a friend, and one of them will help guide me to the answer that was there all along.

I wish every mother knew that their intuition will unfold and guide them. The outside world can influence you and educate you, but in the end, the answers to everything lie in the relationship between you and your baby.

"

Greer Kirshenbaum, PhD
Neuroscientist, doula, infant sleep specialist
and mother of one

EDWINA'S STORY

My passage into motherhood was equal parts joyful and terrifying.

When I was seven months pregnant, I had a strong sense that we would be the parents of a very sick child. I remember the look on my husband's face when I shared this with him, and his response to 'never wish such a thing upon us'.

It was, of course, not a wish. Rather, a deep feeling about our path ahead. I was convinced that this would be our future.

As the months followed, we welcomed our beautiful Francesca. It was instant love. After enduring the typical newborn haze, at four weeks, I knew something wasn't right. Feeding became difficult, she was grunting in her sleep, and her tummy was enlarged.

The maternal health nurse told me it was gas and bloating, and not to worry. My concerns were simply put down to 'new to parenting'. Her conclusion left me uneasy. So, in the days that followed, I used every opportunity to consult other medical professionals.

The cumulative medical advice should have given me confidence that everything was okay. But as Francesca's health continued to deteriorate, my conviction grew stronger. I demanded the paediatrician organise an emergency ultrasound. It was a Friday afternoon, with little chance of finding an appointment, but I insisted.

At the appointment, the sonographer told us Francesca had ascites (fluid in the abdominal cavity). My hand was trembling trying to google it on my phone. For the second time that week, we made our way back to the children's hospital. This time with the evidence in our hands.

I'll never forget the flurry around our baby girl upon arriving at the emergency department. Nor will I forget the endless attempts to extract a blood sample from her tiny limbs, and the bruising that slowly emerged over her fragile body. All I wanted was to feed my baby girl. But all I could do was sit, wait, and hold her little hand.

By the time the haematologist entered our room that night, the flow of clinicians ceased and there was a weary calmness in the air. As my husband clasped my hand, we listened to the words no parent should ever have to hear: '... your daughter has leukaemia, cancer.' Within seconds, my legs gave way, and I was on the floor. In that moment, the fabric of our lives changed forever.

At five weeks of age, Francesca was formally diagnosed with acute megakaryoblastic leukaemia (AMKL), a very rare leukaemia. She was given only a small chance of survival. Within days she started an intensive chemotherapy treatment, supported by leading global experts and research. Finally, my baby girl was getting the medical attention she needed.

The hardest of days followed diagnosis – we almost lost Francesca multiple times. During that time, my mind travelled to the darkest of places. Were we doing the right thing by hooking our baby girl up to chemotherapy? Was all the pain and suffering worth it, given the odds against us? Were we strong enough to fight this bloody disease alongside our daughter? Will our marriage survive the trial ahead? It was a scary place to be.

Despite the terror and self-doubt, I knew I had to overcome the trauma of diagnosis. I had to focus on what I could control and embrace the motherhood given to me. I only needed to take one look at my fighting Frankie, and I was inspired to be the best mum I could be.

I was determined to breastfeed Francesca throughout her treatment, despite every hurdle. It was as much for her nourishment as it was for my mental wellbeing. I loved the way her hand glided over my breast, beckoning her contentment. When she was too weak to suck, I cradled her on my chest while the milk trickled down her nasogastric tube. These days were tough, but I was always filled with comfort knowing I was sustaining her with my liquid gold. When she was ready, with love and patience, we always found our way back together.

For six months, Francesca was an inpatient at the children's hospital. I slept by her side every night, listening to the beeping rhythm of hospital machines, and nurses' footsteps down the hall. My husband was our rock, travelling from home every day to be with us. Together, we learnt to be parents in the confines of a hospital room. We navigated the constant flow of medical staff and procedures. We managed our big emotions. And amidst the madness, we found space for family life.

The Motherhood Space

Most importantly, we battled childhood cancer. After her first round of chemotherapy, Francesca exceeded all medical expectations and achieved remission. Based on her initial diagnosis, we never imagined such a result. We battled the disease over another three rounds of chemotherapy, each one bringing greater certainty of a brighter future. In the marathon we were running, nothing would have been possible without our medical team, and the unwavering support of family and friends.

Today, Francesca is a thriving little girl. Her life is made even more extraordinary by the obstacles she has faced. Her health is monitored regularly, and as each year passes, we are filled with hope. Her life is my greatest joy.

I never thought I had the strength to bring another baby into this crazy world. For years, I even struggled to enjoy the presence of other babies. It triggered a pain so deep. Only recently, since the arrival of our second baby girl, I feel I can stop mourning the parenthood I never got. For the first time, our second daughter Florence is helping me enjoy the normalcy of motherhood, and is creating a family dynamic that is richer than ever.

With this joy, comes the constant reminder of pain. Strangely, I don't want this pain to go, as it is a great reminder of my inner strength. It brings me comfort, that together, my little family can conquer anything that lies ahead.

Edwina Lee, human resources leader and mother of Francesca and Florence

Feeding

I am two years into my third breastfeeding journey and can safely say it has been the hardest thing I have ever done.

Not just in motherhood. Ever. Before I share my story I want to acknowledge you, incredible mother, for however you fed your babies. You are my hero. Breastfeeding is hard! It can be painful, exhausting, time-consuming and stressful, it feels impossible with toddlers underfoot and a distracted baby, there are endless hurdles and sometimes it's just too much. But! It can also be wonderful, joyful, effortless, tender and full of sweet moments you want to bottle forever. No two journeys are the same and every woman should be celebrated for however hers unfolds.

I think the challenge for so many mothers is that we are bombarded with messages like 'breast is best' and 'breastfeeding is free' while at the same time given little or no support (funded or otherwise) to meet our breastfeeding goals. Breast is only best if it's best for the mother as well as her baby, if her mental health is stable and she is given an exceptional amount of support to sustain her – partners who show up, paid parental leave, breastfeeding education, lactation consultants, childcare, food, sleep, rest, encouragement. For most, I don't think it's possible without this minimum level of care. And breastfeeding is only free if we don't value a mother's time or what it costs to hire the help she may need.

The World Health Organization and many national breastfeeding bodies recommended breastfeeding until the age of two and beyond. I understand the need for these recommendations but they are redundant in the absence of, at the very least, paid government leave, free breastfeeding education and postpartum support. Putting this message out into the world without practical and financial care for families only serves to make mothers feel guilty if they did not meet their breastfeeding goals. Like so many things in motherhood, we take the blame when the blame should be placed squarely on the shoulders of society and government and their lack of support for mothers and families, which should be recognised globally as healthcare and healthcare is a human right. If you do hope to breastfeed and are financially able to afford it, hire a lactation consultant during your pregnancy so you have someone you know to support you in the first hours, days and weeks of your journey. There is so much conflicting and confusing advice out there and often so many hurdles in the early days that having one trusted source of information can take the pressure off and allow you to feel fully supported as you and your baby find your way.

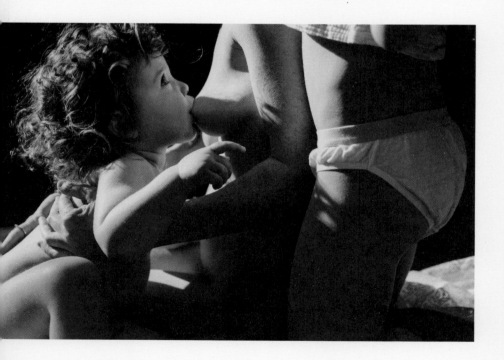

Try to think beyond the birth during pregnancy – good antenatal education that includes postpartum is key to a successful breastfeeding journey. It can be hard as a midwife to explain the what, whys and hows of early breastfeeding in the days after birth when oxytocin is flooding a new mother's brain, making it difficult for her to absorb complex information. It's also really important to know that medical interventions can potentially impact breastfeeding success. Medications used during labour, induction, epidural, caesarean – these can all make babies sleepy and lead to ineffective feeding in the first few days, which in turn impacts a mother's milk volume. That of course doesn't mean that breastfeeding is doomed, it just means that extra lactation support is probably going to be needed to ensure good stimulation of the breasts by other means, like expressing frequently until baby can do it themselves. It's so important to lay down these essential early foundations to get breastfeeding off to a good start.

"

Katie James
Midwife and IBCLC lactation consultant

Before becoming a mother, I thought breastfeeding would naturally work out. It did, and it didn't. My only preparation before Camille was born was a trip to the Upper Breast Side to be fitted for maternity bras and be told by the matriarch owner that I was having a boy (she'd never been wrong, apparently). I also bought a breast pump and nipple cream but other than that, I went in totally blind. Camille latched minutes after she was born, my milk came in two days later and she fed nonstop until we left the hospital on day three. I thought we were doing well until we met with the hospital's lactation consultant just before leaving.

I was all packed up and ready to go. She entered the room, told me I was doing it all wrong, gave me a nipple shield, checked a box on my chart and left. I'd never been so confused. At home, I started to overthink things. I got an app to track her feeds and we fumbled our way through those first few weeks. I felt tense before every feed and the nipple pain was unbearable. Camille was happy and settled and putting on weight but I couldn't relax. At around ten weeks, she started refusing the breast. Overnight feeds were fine but as soon as the sun came up, the battle began. She just didn't seem to want to feed at all. I persevered for two weeks through tears but in the end she preferred the bottle so I started pumping for all but her overnight feeds and continued until she was fifteen months old.

I felt grief for not being able to breastfeed her. And the experience of exclusively pumping almost broke me mentally and physically, but I did it because I wanted her to have my milk and I wanted to keep feeding her overnight because I needed that time and connection with her. I went back to work when she was so little and those overnight feeds, just her and I on the couch overlooking our fire escape and the city beyond, were magic. It was a rocky road and not at all how I imagined it to be, but we navigated it together.

Audrey was born two years and ten months after Camille and just like her big sister, she fed beautifully in the beginning and then started refusing the breast around ten weeks of age. I panicked. I tried everything. Nothing worked. She also fed well overnight but only occasionally during the day, if the room was dark and she was sleepy and there was no noise – not the easiest conditions to create with a toddler in tow. I have since learnt breast refusal and needing a dark quiet room are common experiences around this age but I didn't know that at the time. And so, against everything I knew was right for my mental health, I went back to pumping and continued until Audrey was also fifteen months old. Camille watched so much *Peppa Pig* during that time she had an English accent for most of her third year of life and still calls training wheels 'stabilisers'. After almost three years of daily use, my pump stopped working around the time I finished feeding Audrey. The girls and I decided to have a ceremonial smashing before putting it in the bin – it had affected our lives that much.

When Freddie was born, I knew logistically, physically, emotionally and mentally that I would not and could not pump for him if it came to that. If he also refused the breast, we'd embrace formula or donor milk. I needed to finally take the pressure off and enjoy breastfeeding him for as long as it lasted. Surrendering to that was healing in itself.

Freddie was the biggest of our three babies at 3.6 kg, and he was born hungry. He fed beautifully in the beginning, just like the girls, and around ten weeks he also started refusing the breast. This time I didn't panic. His weight was steady and I felt confident that together we'd find our way, whatever it was. I rested. I ate. I asked James to take time off work so we could get back on track. We did lots of skin-to-skin. Eventually, he started searching for my breast again and is still feeding two years later. Some days I am exhausted and feel ready to stop, but then he pats the couch and says, 'Mama, milk', and we cuddle and he slows down for a minute in his busy day and we both rest. Sometimes he doesn't even want to drink, he just loves the closeness of resting his cheek on my breast.

I think we'll wean soon, although I am not sure how to do that, having never had to do it before. The last few weeks he has not wanted his night feed but still likes me to take my top off so he can lay his head on my chest to fall asleep. And the last few mornings he has said, 'No milk mama', when I offer it to him. So I think he might be doing it all on his own.

EMILY'S STORY

I was so fortunate to breastfeed both my beautiful sons for two and a half years each. It was an absolute pillar of my parenting, until it wasn't anymore.

I weaned my first son when I was a few months pregnant with my second baby. I planned a trip away and spent three days reading, sleeping and eating. My hormones were already all over the shop being in early pregnancy and I didn't really notice much mood change. When I came home he asked for 'milkies' a few times and soon moved on. It was easier than I had imagined.

My second son is a different story. After close to two years I was ready to stop. A friend asked if I was really ready to wean or if I was in need of more support. It was a good question; I think we can get frustrated feeding active toddlers and babies, but maybe what we need is more boundaries, support in the home or help with our kids? I was always terrible with feeding boundaries, and always had a boob hanging out.

The lead up to weaning was difficult for me. It was almost impossible to imagine life without feeding. How will he get to sleep? How will I comfort him? How will we sleep at night? Am I ready to detach from my baby in this way? I knew he was my last baby so it felt especially hard knowing I would probably never feed again.

I wanted a conscious weaning process where there was space to process our feelings around it. In the week leading up, I took lots of photos and we baked a chocolate cake to mark the beginning of weaning. While we made it, I talked to my children about our feeding journeys, how much I had loved it, how difficult it could be and I thanked them for doing it with me. I then explained why I was ready to stop. Once the cake was ready, we lit candles and they sang happy birthday to my boobs! It was nice to bring some fun and levity to the process.

We night weaned first. I slept with our eldest while our kids' father took charge of night-time parenting our youngest. We read a book called *Nursies When the Sun Shines*, I drank the Mama Goodness Slow Your Flow Tea and took their weaning drops – I love having rituals to support myself through transitions.

After a week of night weaning the kids' father took them away for a night and I had a dreamy twenty-four hours alone. I wanted to create some artwork to help process my final weaning journey and this felt so good as I hadn't had time to make any work for years. I played beautiful music, made marks with oil pastels and had a good cry. I also planned a weaning ceremony for myself. Five years of nursing

The Motherhood Space

feels monumental and I really wanted to honour my body and be surrounded by people in my life who have supported me through this journey. I've saved some milk I pumped which I will return to the earth and a small amount to possibly make a breastmilk keepsake ring.

A few weeks after weaning, my eldest son started his first year of primary school, a huge adjustment for us all. I noticed I was having a tough time and felt really down, irritable, unmotivated and then I lost my appetite. I realised that it probably wasn't completely due to my son starting school but the emotionally taxing transition was exacerbating the deeper feelings I was having after weaning. I scoured the internet for stories and stumbled across the term 'post weaning depression'. Once I realised I was most likely experiencing this I was able to step back and remind myself that my body was probably working really hard to bring my hormones back in balance. I started speaking to other parents and found comfort in hearing their experiences. I began taking herbs to help support my body and hormones. A few weeks later I was coping better and starting to feel the glimmers of hope and excitement again. It was a real rollercoaster and something that I don't think is given enough airtime. If I was ever to wean again I'd try to go slower to lessen the hormone crash. I'd also prepare for extra support after weaning; more meals in the freezer, I'd take naturopathic herbs earlier and maybe a few days away from family life to drop back into my body.

Emily Williamson, postpartum doula and mother of Jimmy and Jack

FAIRLEIGH'S STORY

The formula feeding journey of my identical twin boys was more painful than I ever thought possible. I didn't realise how much I actually wanted to be able to breastfeed them until I couldn't. With limited supply and hungry, premature babies I mix-fed with great difficulty, feeling a sense of disappointment every time I scooped formula into their bottles after yet another failed pumping session. At the time, I truly believed that formula was toxic for them, a feeling that was imparted on me by the general public, staff in the Special Care unit at the hospital and misled maternal child health nurses. I now realise how wrong they were. My boys have been exclusively formula fed since ten weeks of age and couldn't be healthier or happier. I still feel anger about how the professionals made me feel and I think I will always feel a sense of regret for the time I lost, sitting strapped to the pump, trying desperately to increase my supply while missing those precious newborn days.

Fairleigh McLaren, teacher and mother of Kit and Parker

The Motherhood Space

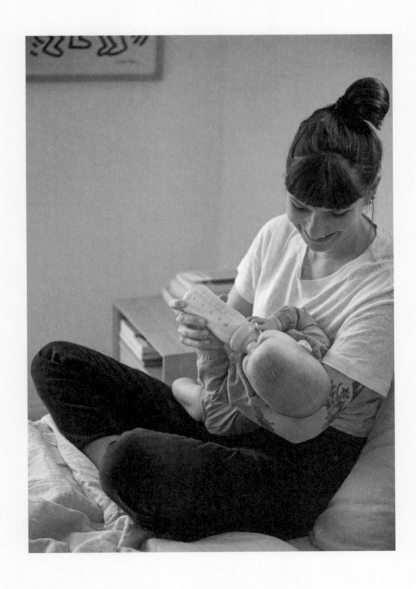

Sleep

We have a cultural obsession with sleep.

It feels controversial to even be wading into this space but I am going there for two reasons: it is the number one thing the families I support want to talk about postpartum; and the societal pressure put on parents to have a baby who 'sleeps well' robs us of so much joy in the first year of a baby's life and beyond.

'Are they sleeping through the night yet?' has got to be one of the most common and misguided questions asked of new families. As a society, particularly a western society, we have such unrealistic expectations of what 'normal' newborn and infant sleep looks like – normal in inverted commas because every child is different and their sleep is not linear – and this leads to feelings of guilt and failure if our babies aren't 'sleeping through the night' or napping in their cot at an age when it is actually potentially dangerous for them to be doing so. Every baby is different with different sleep needs and we have to get to know our own children and trust our gut when making decisions about what is best for them – not looking to or comparing ourselves to others or what the cultural noise and unregulated sleep training industry is saying and guilting us into. If your best friend has an excellent sleeper and you don't, it's not because they are doing everything right and you are doing everything wrong. It is the literal luck of the draw – we have three children, all with different temperaments that manifest in vastly different sleep needs and I have been very humbled and learnt a lot from our journey (more on page 111).

It is biologically normal and necessary for newborns to wake multiple times a night and, if you are breastfeeding, these overnight feeds are important for building and sustaining milk supply. Most older babies and toddlers and children and teenagers (and adults!) will also wake at night – we're just not wired to sleep without a peep for eight to twelve hours straight. It's also absolutely fine to breastfeed or rock or bounce or walk or drive or stroll your baby to sleep and you're not spoiling them if you choose to do so, sometimes it is the only thing that works. You are not failing if you put your baby down 'drowsy but awake' but they don't settle on their own – most babies will not do this. Contact naps are biologically normal and important for mother–baby bonding, co-regulation and creating a secure attachment – most newborns will not sleep well in a room alone away from you and it breaks my heart to see mothers spending hours and hours in dark rooms patting and shushing and trying to resettle their babies and feeling like they are failing if they don't get them sleeping in a cot and on a strict schedule by a certain age. Most of the time it's not possible and up until the age of six months it's potentially dangerous – SIDS guidelines say that babies should always sleep in a room with an adult until at least the age of six months.

But of course we all need to sleep, so what to do?

Every family and every baby is different and you need to find what works for you, ensuring it's a team effort. If you have a partner, they should be just as involved as you are. Tag-team sleep in the early months so you're both getting periods of rest and have your partner do the settling if you're breastfeeding but not feeding to sleep. Many parents choose to co-sleep and if you follow the guidelines to decrease the risk factors (see www.rednose. org.au to read these in detail), it is safe and you might find everyone gets a bit more sleep. If you are looking for co-sleeping resources I recommend James J McKenna.

I can't have a chapter on sleep without mentioning sleep training. There is so much noise in this space and a lot of it is very black and white: either you sleep train or you don't. I have come to learn that it is nuanced and most families exist somewhere in the grey – especially in the west where there is often a sole parent at home juggling a thousand things with little, if any, support, or both parents are working and their children are in care. As with everything in parenthood, you do you. There is so much cultural pressure to sleep train it almost feels like an expectation – as if there is no alternative. Actually, not sleep training is absolutely a valid option so if you love holding your baby all day and co-sleeping and feeding through the night and it's working for you, keep doing what you're doing. If you are considering sleep training, like everything, do your research and trust your gut – if it doesn't feel right, stop. Be wary of strict one-size-fits-all schedules, harsh approaches (there are many alternatives to crying-it-out) and anyone who tells you a baby's needs have been met if they are fed, clean and dry; completely disregarding the very basic human needs for touch, safety, reassurance and connection – it's an industry that feeds on the cultural pressure of having a baby who sleeps, with the implication that you are doing something wrong if your baby isn't. I promise, you're not.

Here's a little of our sleep journey ...

Before little Fred came along, we'd had it pretty easy. Camille and Audrey both sleep well – Audrey in particular, she has always loved and needed a lot of sleep and as a little girl would get her dummies, grab my hand and say, 'Bed, mama', and fall asleep within minutes. I can remember only a handful of nights in Camille's first month or so when she was unsettled. James worked out that if he sang 'Wetsuit' by The Vaccines and rocked her in a particular way she'd stop crying. Now every time I hear that song I'm immediately taken back to milk-soaked sheets and those hazy newborn days. Camille napped well too, never in a cot, always on someone. Mum and Dad came over from Australia for her first couple of months and my sisters were also living in New York so there was always someone for her to cosy into. It was a true village and I know how lucky I am to have had that support. A couple of weeks before I went back to work, I met with our beautiful nanny Joan who asked me to write down Camille's routine and I remember thinking, what routine? So I spent those weeks doing my best to introduce her to cot naps and wake windows without much success but by the time I went back to work she was slowly getting used to it and about a month later she was happily napping twice a day in her cot.

Because we had a studio apartment, Camille's cot was right by our bed until we moved home to Melbourne just before she turned two. There, she went straight into a bed in her own room. She didn't love it, and woke every night around midnight to come into our bed. She did this nightly until she was six years old, when we set a challenge (bribe?) for her and Audrey, who by this time was also finding her way into our bed every night: if they stayed in their own beds for two weeks straight, we'd buy them bunk beds (I was six months pregnant with Freddie and wasn't sure how we'd go with five in a double bed). I didn't think there was any way they would do it but they did!

Now our girls are eight and five. I still lie with them every night before they fall asleep, which usually takes more than an hour, sometimes two. There are questions and stories and songs and cuddles and back scratching and requests for water and milk and apples. Most nights I tell stories of weekends spent at my grandparents' farm growing up and if they are still not winding down after that, we'll do a meditation (see page 116). Camille sleeps with her blankie that she's had since she was born and that I'm not allowed to wash anymore lest I ruin her smell. Audrey switches teddies every night and it's often an epic quest to find the right one. I really love this time – they tell the best stories at night and give such vivid insights into their busy days – but it's also exhausting, especially if I had very little sleep the night before and the dishes haven't been done and I still have work to do. Still, I try to stay calm when I ask them for the hundredth time to stop talking, then I put a podcast in my ears and usually fall asleep with them, stumbling back out around 9.30 pm. Every night I declare I have never been so tired and yet I'll still stay up for the next few hours because it is the only time in my day when nothing is asked of me and the house is quiet and I can watch a show or take a bath.

Freddie, bless him, has been a wild ride. I knew there was no chance we'd be lucky enough to have three 'good' sleepers. He was unsettled for the first couple of months and cried every time we lay him down, so James and I – and my life-saving mum – took turns holding him upright all night long until he was about ten weeks old. He would cluster feed until about 9 pm, then James would take him and I'd sleep until about 1 am, then feed him and hold him again until around 5 am when James would take him and I'd try to get a couple more hours sleep before the girls woke. I was so tired during this time I would hallucinate and felt disconnected to everything going on around us. Around three months of age he started to settle and sleep without us holding him but would still wake anywhere from four to forty-four times a night. He napped on me during the day when I could fit it in around the girls' drop-offs and pick-ups but his only real solid chunk of day sleep was between 5 pm and 8 pm when James would get home from work, wrap him up in the sling and walk the streets of our neighbourhood.

Freddie is now two and sleeps in the little nook under James's arm once reserved for me. He still wakes often and it's not unheard of for us to be playing trains or making playdough at 4 am. I recently moved into the spare bed in the girls' room, initially to night wean him but it feels kind of permanent (for now) since we're all getting more sleep. I wasn't sure about this move at first but after some research I've learnt it is very common for couples to sleep separately during this intense period of parenting little ones – whatever gets everyone more sleep!

Since he was little, James has done all of Freddie's overnight settling, bringing him to me to breastfeed and then bouncing, rocking, patting, shushing and cuddling him back to sleep, often for hours. Last month he was away for work and Freddie woke before I went to bed. I walked in and reached my arms out to him and he said, 'No, Mama. Dada!' It was the first time any of our children had ever asked for Daddy over me. I felt sad and relieved.

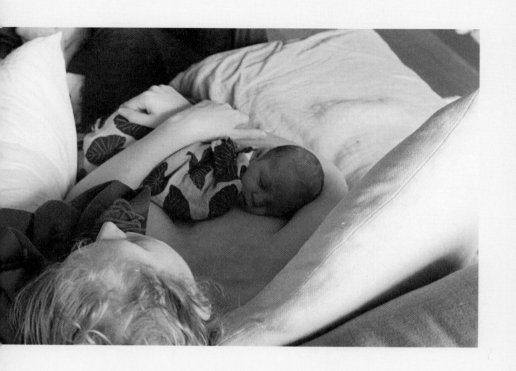

We are totally unprepared for what normal infant sleep looks like. We're conditioned to think we'll be able to rock our babies to sleep and put them in the crib and walk away. If that's not how it plays out for you then we have this narrative that our baby is controlling us or we're a bad parent or we're not doing enough and it breaks my heart to see this preoccupation because it can so quickly spiral into anxiety and depression. Education is key. It's a giant myth that your baby will sleep through the night and nap in a room alone. The guidelines say babies should be in the same room as you for at least a few months for night-time and for naps, and I don't think anyone knows that naps are included in that. Frequent waking is completely normal and necessary for so many reasons. People think their baby is going to sleep through the night by a few months old when it's probably not going to happen until two-and-a-half or three and even then there is a huge spectrum of sleep needs and contact needs in children. Some are going to want to be in the same room and sleeping close to their parents and waking for comfort until they are six or eight and sometimes into their teenage years and that is normal and healthy and the reality for so many families. The important thing is to ensure both parents – if there are two parents – are involved in supporting their child's sleep development from the beginning so both parents feel supported and the whole family is getting rest.

"

Greer Kirshenbaum, PhD
Neuroscientist, doula, infant sleep specialist
and mother of one

A bedtime ritual

After eight years of settling children to sleep every single night, I have found two tricks that work (almost) every time. The first is storytelling. I have taken my girls on many of my childhood adventures of weekends spent at my grandparents' farm. They want to hear about the crazy haystack slides and the terrifying geese and outdoor toilet and my nanny's veggie soup that I devoured thousands of times during my eight years of vegetarianism only to later find out that she boiled beef bones for the stock. I always end with how safe and warm my body felt sinking into the old beds at night, and how my mum would come and tuck me in and pull the crochet knit blanket up to my chin. Audrey is often asleep by this point. Camille's busy mind takes a little longer to wind down and she'll fight sleep for as long as she can, often falling asleep mid-sentence.

So I'll use my second trick: meditation. We'll lie on our backs with our hands on our belly and close our eyes. We imagine our bodies getting heavy and pretend to fall through soft clouds. We imagine all our worries falling through those clouds too, so we don't have to think about them as we fall asleep. We'll breathe in slowly and out slowly, feeling our tummies rise. We'll relax every part of our body, from the tip of our head to our little toes. We end by naming all the people in our lives who we love and who love us. It's so grounding and the perfect end to the day – if you have the patience for it (which I promise you I don't always).

Growing

One day soon you will look down at your baby and all of a sudden they won't feel so small anymore. Almost overnight they've become a toddler, then a child, then a tween and time that once stood still is now flying by and you think, wait, hold on, I'm not quite ready for this all to move so fast. This is the season of growth and change. A new dynamic for your family. More time for yourself as you move out of babyhood and come up for air and try to remember what moves you and lights you up inside. It is still a season of sacrifice and chaos and very early mornings and maybe more babies as you grow your family and your heart but mostly this season is about coming out of the fog and learning the lessons that come as your children grow, the greatest and hardest of which is realising that motherhood is as much about letting go as it is holding on. There is grief and relief as you move through these years and your children seek and find their own way without you. Like all seasons of motherhood, this season of growth will bring you to your knees and call you to rise again and again and again. Look for and hold on to the joy to be found in the simplest of moments and give yourself grace always.

Loneliness and finding time to be alone

When you become a mother you're never really alone again and yet, sometimes, you've never felt so alone. It's one of the great dichotomies of motherhood.

There are a lot of lonely parts, especially in the early days before your children can talk and play and when it feels impossible to leave the house even if it's just to meet friends at the park. It is common to feel isolated within our communities – we don't reach out for help and company as much as we maybe should and sometimes it feels as if we don't have anyone to reach out to. We don't live in villages the way we were designed to, so it can be hard to ever feel fully connected and witnessed on your journey.

When I was a new mother in New York City, I would look out our windows at night and there were always lights on in the other apartments no matter what time it was. I would hear voices on the street, sirens blaring and the endless white noise of the city and I truly never felt alone – it was a gift to be initiated into motherhood in this way. It wasn't until we were back home in Melbourne with a toddler and a newborn that I first felt the pangs of loneliness I'd heard mothers speak of. The days were quiet and long, breastfeeding wasn't working out, James left for work early and came home late, it would often take all morning to get the girls and me out of bed and down the stairs, and Camille was still too young to talk to in a way that brings us both so much joy today.

I remember taking Audrey to her one-month wellness check at the maternal child health nurse and the nurse asking me if I'd been placed in a mothers' group yet. 'No,' I said. 'But that sounds great!' 'Oh, that's right,' she said. 'It's because Audrey is your second baby. We only have groups for first-time mothers.' I was too tired to protest and left feeling rejected. No groups for second-time mothers? Does everyone else know what they're doing? Have they all made their mum friends? Have I missed the boat?

On the days I felt particularly lost I'd take myself back to those nights in New York looking out over the lights of the city. I'd imagine the apartments were filled with the millions of other mothers feeding and rocking and soothing and holding and playing with their babies and toddlers and children and it brought a sense of comfort I'm not quite sure how to explain. Perhaps it was the community I was craving, that even though I couldn't sit beside these women I could still sense them there alongside me.

Today I don't feel lonely in the way I once did. My children are older and they are such great company and the one silver lining of the pandemic is having James home a lot more. Even though he is working, having another adult in the house brings a huge sense of comfort and companionship. Today I find myself craving more time alone as I come out of the fog of Freddie's first two sleepless years of life and can almost catch a glimpse of the next season of my motherhood journey. I say almost because I am still deeply in this intense caregiving phase and also clinging to the possibility of one more baby (see page 144), but at the same time can sense a little bit more space opening up for me to find what I want to do next – to re-engage with life and rediscover what lights me up beyond caring for my children.

What I know I must do now is prioritise finding that space and keeping it for myself. It shouldn't, but it almost feels as if it's a sacred act – to have alone time to do exactly as I please. To rest without guilt! Like so many mothers, my small pockets of 'me time' are crammed in the middle of a million other things and I simply don't think to prioritise it. When a new pub recently opened just down the road from our house, opposite a supermarket, James was very happy and said he looked forward to a beer on the way to doing our weekly shop. I was aghast – seriously?! 'I would never think to do that,' I said. 'I know,' he replied. 'Maybe you should.' And he's absolutely right. All parents need time alone to breathe and reset – fathers are just typically a lot better at prioritising it.

Time alone to rest, create, exercise, meet friends and simply do as we please is critical for mothers and we have to get better at actively investing in ourselves and in this real need and not apologising for it or feeling guilty about it. There will always be something else we could be doing and a cultural expectation that we, as mothers, put everyone before ourselves, but if we continue that way, we'll burn out and everyone will suffer. Make space for time alone to do whatever feels good to you because you matter and this act of self-preservation matters.

One of the most challenging parts of motherhood for me is finding how I can come up for air and get time for myself. I love solitude, I love having an hour-long hot bath, I love laying in bed and watching a movie and I love my work but I find it challenging to be the present mum I want to be and also follow what lights me up.

"

Juliet Allen
Sexologist and mother of Milli and Sol

Firsts, lasts and letting go

I had a thought the other night as I was wading through the washing: when will I fold our very last onesie? We only have a few that still fit Freddie and I find myself trying to squeeze him into them as if desperately trying to hold on to his littleness.

Maybe there will be another baby? Maybe not? But even so, there will come a day when we're not washing onesies anymore and that does something to my heart I can't quite explain. When I see a pregnant woman or hear a newborn cry I think, wasn't that me, just yesterday? It's as if, all of a sudden, I'm on the other side looking in on a life that I thought was still mine but every day I am getting further and further away from. I'm not ready yet. I'm not ready to let go of this season. I thought it would last longer. I thought it might last forever.

A common narrative on motherhood is that it gets easier as our children get older. That they will eventually potty train and feed themselves and walk without running onto the road at every opportunity and play independently and read all on their own and maybe even start to sleep all night – and all of these milestones mean they need us less and less. But is that easier? Physically, yes. Emotionally, that's harder to answer. There is no greater joy than watching our children grow and learn and explore and wonder and question, but with that joy is the knowledge that they are ever so slowly moving away from us and deeper into their own world, their own identity, their own friendships, and we're not always going to be there to be a part of that journey or to fix things for them or to protect them or hold them when they are sad, and that physically hurts to think about. Today I am their moon and their stars, but I know they will ever so slowly drift away from me and create a world that I will of course still be a part of but won't always be the centre of. And that's wonderful – it's what we want – and it breaks my heart at the same time. I'm worried I'll make mistakes and because of those mistakes I might lose them a little more. I want to pull them in so tight but also want to see them soar, as I know they will. I am only just beginning to grasp the meaning of all this as I see it play out before my eyes, as my Grade 2 girl moves from child to tween and I watch in awe as she tries to make sense of all that is changing for her. Eight years old feels so big, in a way that four felt so big and one felt so big and one month felt so big, once upon a time. It's a constant state of mourning and celebrating simultaneously. I have so much reverence for this season and I am learning ever so slowly to let go of the children we have today and look forward to the teenagers and adults they will become but it's also really hard. It's bittersweet. I'm not sure there's ever been a better use for that expression.

Letting go for the very first time and learning to trust that our children will be happy and safe in the care of others is, in my experience, one of the hardest rites of passage of motherhood. When Camille was two, I got a part-time job and she started childcare two days a week. It wasn't the first time I had left her, that was back in New York when she was four months old and I returned to work and she was cared for full time by our nanny Joan. We'd only met Joan a few weeks earlier but I had a gut feeling that all would be well and didn't worry as much as I thought I would with Camille in her care. Joan turned out to be an angel and we were very lucky to have her as part of our village for a moment in time.

Leaving Camille at childcare was different. It broke our hearts and hers. She was never happy and cried at every drop-off for almost two years. They always said she settled but she told me otherwise – whip smart and articulate from the age of eighteen months, she'd tell me all the reasons she didn't like it over dinner each night: the spaghetti tasted funny and the day was too long and the teachers didn't answer her questions and sometimes Blankie would go missing and it took forever for me to come through the door and she missed me. I listened and validated her concerns and told her I was so sad to be away from her as well and that while work was also important to me, and important for our family, I would try to come through the door a little earlier tomorrow. I think about her days there often and I still feel guilty about leaving her. In hindsight she was in the wrong place and I wish we'd moved her. Audrey and Freddie have also spent time at childcare and have both thrived with the lovely carers we feel very lucky to have found for them.

The gradual lack of control that is forced upon you as your baby grows into a child and that child into an adult scares me. The desire to keep Poppy safe and happy is overwhelming and the thought that I won't always be able to do that is terrifying. At the time of writing we are navigating the beginning of daycare and learning to trust that she will be safe in the arms of others. It feels like the beginning of learning to let go.

"

Beth Ryan
Midwife and mother of Poppy

Some children love childcare from day one while others take longer to settle away from their parents and home. Like us, millions of families around the world depend on public or private childcare programs to enable both parents to return to work. We're fortunate to live in Australia where government childcare subsidies do exist. You may live in a country where the subsidies are far better or non-existent, you may live in a place where any type of childcare is a privilege. Globally, we need to do better – we need safe, affordable care for our children so we can financially support our families and progress our careers. But, no matter where you live or what type of childcare is available to you, leaving our babies at any age is a hard transition.

When Camille started kindergarten at four years old she was very hesitant to go. Her experience of childcare was still very present and it was hard for her, and for me, to let go. One of her teachers, who was older and assured me she knew best, told me to drop her and run and ignore her cries, and that this approach would build the resilience she would need for school. I took a different approach and stayed with Camille for as long as she needed me to, sometimes hours. Audrey spent so much time there she was in the official kinder photos. Little by little, Camille grew more comfortable in her surroundings and by term four she was skipping in, happy and at ease. All in her own time. I learnt that sometimes you need to hold on a little longer before you let go.

The night before Camille started school a few months later, she wore her uniform to bed and told us she was most excited about lunch orders and most nervous about making new friends. The next day, she walked confidently into her classroom, no tears, and hasn't looked back.

I know there will be more letting go. I don't think it ever ends. And I probably won't get any better at it. I can see myself years from now, sobbing uncontrollably as they leave our home one by one for university or travel or to move in with friends or boyfriends or girlfriends. I'll hold them tight as if by some miracle the force of my love will change their minds and they'll decide to stay. I know rationally that all of this growing up and being independent of us is what is supposed to happen and I love it and am thankful for all of it, but it's still hard. It still hurts.

Ever since Camille was two and telling me over dinner that she was unhappy at childcare, I have been working on making sure our home is a soft place to land for our children. I remind them every day they are safe here and we love them and there is nothing they can't tell us. I think it is so easy to doubt yourself as a parent and to question whether you are doing enough to help them and guide them, if you're making the right decisions or the wrong ones, if you're stepping in at the right times and also stepping back to give them space to make their own mistakes. It's never easy but if they are loved and have that soft place to land then I do believe everything will be okay in the end.

Stand up for your child, because there isn't anyone else who will. Trust that you can be their advocate and fight for them and if you feel something's not quite right, explore that.

"

Dr Hazel Keedle
Midwife, author, researcher and mother of five

The worry that comes with raising a child, protecting them, keeping them safe and guiding them, all while encouraging them to flourish as their own little person, has been the most unexpected element of mothering for me.

"

Kate Bloom
Birth and postpartum doula and
mother of Jozie, Pixie and Dusty

Slow days and simple joys

There was a time a few years ago, when Camille was five and Audrey was two, that it felt for a while like time stood still.

It was just the three of us day after day and we'd spend our mornings walking, no place to be. I'd get coffee and let Camille lead the way. We'd eventually end up at the park after stopping to smell (and pick) every flower and pat every dog. I can still remember how the very early morning sun would bounce off their skin. The air was cold and the day ahead was long. Life soon got busy again as I took on more projects and opened my business, but for those few months we all took a big deep breath in and a long slow breath out. I miss those days.

A few weeks ago, out of the blue, Camille asked me to bake the cookies I used to take with us on those walks. 'Can we go back to that time when we'd just walk to the park and have nothing else to do?' she said.

Now Camille is eight, Audrey is five and Freddie is two. They are growing so fast it feels like our house is shrinking. I have a feeling that years from now, as my teenagers race out the door, I will long for the days I am in now just as much as I long for those mornings at the park. I will yearn for their wild imaginations and their endless questions like, what is the biggest animal in the ocean and how long is the day and how long is the night and how far away are the stars and can we visit the stars and why can't we visit the stars? Most of all, I will long for the way they scream 'Muuuuuummyyyyy!' as I walk in the door. The way they run at me from all directions and hang onto my knees and my waist as I shuffle inside, each one with a hundred stories to tell. The joy of coming home to them is the simplest and most perfect thing I have ever experienced.

Mothers are often told to enjoy every moment because it passes us by so quickly. I'm not going to tell you that – we both know it's not possible. There are hard days and long days and days apart and lonely days and nonstop-fighting days and days where you will shout a lot. And then there are the perfectly ordinary wonder-filled days in the middle of all the madness, when nothing and everything happens and you make a silent deal with yourself to never forget how they got lost in their games, or chose a book from the shelf and shuffled backwards all the way to the couch and up into your lap, or fell asleep mid-sentence because they just had so much to tell you and there was never enough time in the day for all their stories. Hold on to these days and when you have the time and the mental space and the patience, let them lead the way. Take photos – and make sure you're in some of them. Write down memories and the funny things they say. Keep their drawings. Linger a little longer. They can feel so long but we all know they won't last forever, these never-ending days.

I love the way motherhood transforms mundanity into moments that make you wish time would stand still. Watching Poppy scoop food into her mouth, seeing her and my partner cuddle on the couch, observing her watch the world pass by from her pram – all of it gives me a full feeling in my chest, a feeling of deep contentment.

"

Beth Ryan
Midwife and mother of Poppy

MELANIE'S STORY

Among stories of motherdom, you might call mine a worst-case scenario. I certainly would have, had you told me my son wouldn't walk in the way that most children do.

My son, Arlo, has a physical disability that impacts every part of his body. It started with a brain injury at his birth and, after six months of smiles, sweetness and not a single motor milestone met, the official diagnosis – quadriplegic cerebral palsy – came crashing in on a wave of uncertainties.

Back then I was scared, sad and stubbornly unaccepting of my parenthood prognosis. Like I said, you might call it a worst-case scenario.

You – like me – would be spectacularly mistaken. And understandably so.

You see, children are sold to us with standard, built-in features. Parenting books tell us our baby will roll, sit and shuffle into their first steps in a timely fashion. Huggies packaging strongly concurs – babies crawl, toddle and walk their way right out of needing nappies.

That's just how the story goes. And if yours isn't unfolding this way, you try to catch up with the typical narrative. I desperately did, until I started meeting others who'd ventured off-script.

One of them was Debby Elnatan, a fellow mother of a son with cerebral palsy. Debby is the inventor of The Upsee – a nifty device that allows children who can't walk to do so with support – and has spent years researching what she calls 'Broken Child Syndrome'.

In a conversation I would come to feature in my book, *Special: Antidotes to the Obsessions that Come with a Child's Disability*, Debby told me: 'Some parents don't look at their kid's face. They see their arm, their leg, whatever's not working and they want to fix this kid, and meanwhile, they've stolen their childhood.'

One year into Arlo's childhood I was obsessed with him walking. We'd all but moved into his physiotherapy centre and, at home, Arlo was eternally propped against the couch.

'If you have to spend this much energy to get this much progress,' Debby said, spreading her hands wide and then shrinking them in close, 'and meanwhile, their childhood is getting screwed up, is it worth it?'

Debby told me that studies have shown that among adults with disability, mobility is not on the top of their list of priorities. A social life is.

'Okay, so they won't walk, so they'll be in a wheelchair, but are they going to be happy and communicate or are they going to be apathetic and unhappy?' said Debby. 'People are so hung up on walking. It's a trap that everybody falls into – the Broken Child Syndrome – I don't think you can avoid it. The question is, do you ever catch yourself, and get out of it?'

I did, eventually, and wish it hadn't taken writing an entire book to help me do so. This single chapter is unlikely to reassure a parent reeling in the uncertainty of unmet milestones. And yet, the best antidote to my fears, in those early days, was right in front of me.

While I worried that Arlo would never walk, he was working up a wicked sense of humour. While I contemplated stem cell treatments, he was developing an insatiable passion for books and music. While I fretted over him not fitting in, he was effortlessly winning hearts.

Arlo has a knack for crushing preconceived ideas – and misplaced pity – with a single smile.

My baby knew who he was and what he wanted, and I'll forever be grateful for his patience as I fumbled to get with the program. Now deep into this parenthood schtick, I know that walking is not an essential ingredient for a meaningful life. Neither is talking, as we've later discovered.

Beyond the rigid mechanics and marketing of milestones, you get to the guts of what parenting is truly about. Sleep deprivation, immense challenges and extreme, incomprehensible love.

Our firstborn helped us bust parenthood out of its box, so by the time our second came along – in all her medically boring glory – we had a head start. We knew that if you're trying to plot out the future, you're missing the point. You're missing the mayhem and magic that is right here, right now, in this exact moment.

And whatever your version of parenthood is, I can promise you, mayhem and magic are a certainty.

Melanie Dimmitt, freelance journalist, author and mother of Arlo and Odette. Since launching her debut book, *Special: Antidotes to the Obsessions that Come with a Child's Disability*, Melanie has written, spoken, podcasted and advocated far and wide for parents travelling not-so-typical paths.

Surrendering to the chaos

Some days, when I am knee-deep in toys, books and half-eaten toast strewn across the living room floor, there's avocado down my just-washed jeans and a sibling fight is brewing, I wonder, how have I not lost my mind completely? It would take a huge effort to make this much mess and yet somehow my children manage to do it every day before 7 am.

In my eight years of motherhood I have completely lowered my expectations of how tidy our house needs to be and learnt to surrender, little by little, to the chaos. I used to obsess over it and could feel my anxiety rising with each cluttered bench and missing shoe. I'd clean up multiple times a day just for it to be undone in a second. It was exhausting and not worth it. Our children certainly didn't care – who was I doing it for?

I've interrogated this question over the years – why do I care so much? Why can't I wait until the end of the day or even the end of the week to tidy up? Or better still – have James and the kids own it? I think part of it was an urge to have control over something when I felt so out of control in so many other ways. I would also worry that the mess would compound and there would be even more for me to do when the time came. And – the big one – I tied my worth as a mother to it: if I had a clean house then I was doing what a 'good mum' does, wasn't I?

We have been culturally conditioned as mothers to see housework as our domain. It has been this way for generations – we saw our mothers and grandmothers do it and we've internalised the idea that the work of the home is up to us, that if we have a tidy house then at least on the surface we have it together. We really need to start challenging this on a micro family-centred level so our daughters don't internalise the same message and our sons naturally see it as everyone's role to own the work of the home. Housework has to be done, but it shouldn't be the responsibility of one person so that person has to sacrifice their sanity and worth to get it done day after day, hour after hour. Surrender to the chaos and own it as a family. Teach your children from a young age that the work of the home is everyone's responsibility and allow them to witness both parents doing it regardless of who is in paid work and who is not. The only way we're going to get out of this patriarchal trap that has held mothers back for generations is to make changes at home that hopefully, eventually, ever-so-painfully-slowly, filter into our communities and workplaces and governments and the generation we are raising today.

Rituals

I've found one of the best ways to ground myself and my family amidst the chaos is to have simple rituals ebb and flow through our days. I grew up sharing our 'highs and lows' every night during family dinner and now we do it too. We also love Sunday morning pancakes, farm stories at bedtime, Friday night movie night, Women's Weekly cakes made by James each birthday, gingerbread houses that become more elaborate each Christmas and letters written on the eve of their birthdays, which I plan to give them in a big bundle tied with a bow on their eighteenth birthdays. It's so easy to get lost in the chaos of life but these little rituals peppered through our days and years bring such comfort to our lives and to theirs.

Another baby?

Many of us have an idea about how many children we'd eventually like to have but it's not uncommon for that number to change as you start to grow your family and life happens.

There are so many factors to consider when thinking about having another child: the state of your relationship and your finances, the state of the world, sibling dynamics, age, already feeling at capacity and the big one for me right now, having a partner who is not on the same page.

James and I are at a crossroads. A sliding doors scenario in which I imagine both lives and wonder which one will be ours: I would love to have another baby but he is very happy with three. When I was pregnant with Freddie, I thought he would probably be our last baby. I'd always wanted four children but I could see rationally how three made more sense for us. I hoped that when he was born I'd feel done, the way women talk about feeling done. I imagined it would feel like a sense of peaceful completion.

Freddie was just a few days old when I was surprised to once again feel that familiar longing for another baby. I couldn't imagine a world in which I'd never give birth again, or feel my slippery just-born baby skin-to-skin against my body, or be woken by their kicks in the night. Every day that has passed since his birth, while I have watched with joy as he has grown and grasped and crawled and laughed and walked and ran and talked, I have felt an even deeper yearning for another. I cannot fathom that this season of my life is over. That all of a sudden I am on the other side, looking in. Time passed so slowly for my first few years of motherhood that I thought it would be my life forever. But now I am painfully aware that it will end, that it is ending, that the magic and the mess of little children doesn't last and that hurts more than I ever thought possible.

The Motherhood Space

James feels the opposite. He is looking forward to the end of naps and nappies, food strewn across the floor, and a crying baby piercing the silence of the night. But I'm not sure a whole lifetime of being in this moment would be enough, as much as I can also wish the harder days away sometimes – that familiar tension all mothers know well.

It's a painful limbo to be in, wanting another child but knowing your partner doesn't feel the same way. We've spoken about it a lot over the past year but haven't really got anywhere. We ask ourselves how another baby will change our family and change us, and we come up with very different answers. James has said he will come with me on the journey if it is what I want, but if there is to be another baby I need more than that. I need him to want this soul as much as I do and I am not sure he'll get there. And that's heartbreaking. And there is grief. And yet I have also found beauty in this space. I feel at peace knowing that I have spoken my truth, listened to the ache and the yearning and sat with it. I hold space for myself every time I ovulate because to me it feels a little like loss. I feel there is a baby there waiting, but I can't bring myself to call them to us until James is ready. Whatever happens, it feels important to honour this moment in time.

KARA'S STORY

We thought we were done after Jude was born. My husband Charlie and I both felt for a long time that our family was complete. Then in December 2020, something changed. I started having visions of a feminine energy that wanted to join our family. At first I said no, and then I just couldn't say no anymore. I told Charlie. It took him a couple of months and then we opened that door and I got pregnant right away. I'm forty-two, so it's my swansong. I feel emotional about not being pregnant again, about that door closing. As women, we get an opportunity to really be with our mortality in a way that men don't, because we have perimenopause and menopause. Our bodies communicate to us that this part of our lives is over. We go into a kind of descent, and then we get to be with that depth as well as come out the other side; I think that is really beautiful.

We are so excited to meet our baby girl. She's going to be here in less than a month. But none of us know what's coming. There will be a whole recalibration of moving from three to four. I feel nervous about that and I feel grief about it too. I felt it when we were decorating our Christmas tree last year and all of a sudden I had a giant wave of grief realising it was never going to be the three of us doing this together again. I was so aware of things changing and of this ending. And that is parenthood: it's constantly letting go of the people our children were yesterday and embracing the people they are now, again and again and again.

Kara Hoppe, psychotherapist, author, teacher and mother of Jude and Dion

The Motherhood Space

JULIE'S STORY

I thought we were done after two. I have a big age gap – six and eight years between my first two and my second two. I was trying hard to be happy with two. We had a healthy boy and girl and I thought, don't push your luck, be happy with what you've got – which is such a narrative for women: don't be greedy. So instead of really owning my choice, I waited for drunk sex, because then if I got pregnant, it would be as much his 'fault/choice' as mine. Of course, it's flawed thinking. This baby gifted us both with the empowerment that comes with owning your life and choices; at twelve weeks we had a missed miscarriage and the experience broke us both open. Through tears I said to my husband, 'I cannot be seventy and have regret. I'm not here for that. Come with me.' We got on the same page about what was really important to us and had a conscious conception journey from there with our third child, Lola. Then we thought we were done and booked in a vasectomy. On our last hurrah before his procedure the very next day, with me on the second day of my period – who gets pregnant on their full bleeding day the day before a vasectomy?! – we conceived our fourth baby Gwen. It was a difficult pregnancy for me. Lola has additional needs and her journey has been difficult so I spent my whole pregnancy really not sure about a fourth. Gwen's birth was an epic waterbirth and I remember her unfolding like a lotus flower and thinking, 'I spent this whole time not sure if I wanted you or if I could do it, and you just waited for me in this perfection, you waited for me to catch up.' And she is perfect. I think she came for Lola because they have such an exquisite relationship and have needed each other so much. Gwen ties our family together, she is just the most wonderful thing that ever happened to us.

Julie Tenner, intimacy and relationship coach, doula and mother of Heath, Jade, Lola and Gwen

HOLLY'S STORY

I always feared motherhood. I spent my twenties trying to cram in as much as possible, assuming that once I had a child my life would no longer be mine to enjoy. When I met my wonderful partner I confronted my ambivalence and fell pregnant straight away. I was racked with anxiety and my intuition told me something wasn't right. When my GP told me that one in four women miscarry, I knew I'd be one of them. My partner was working overseas when I started bleeding. I birthed a tiny sac at our Melbourne home during the winter, alone.

The months that followed were some of the most transformative of my life. I held space for my grief and treated myself with compassion. I was better at letting go of a pregnancy than having to endure one. When we conceived again, I was incredibly anxious for the first fifteen weeks. After that I was blessed with early kicks that helped to put my mind at rest. I had a healthy pregnancy and an empowering homebirth that left me on a six-week high. After the sleep deprivation and hormonal fallout caught up with me, I fell into a deep postnatal depression combined with insomnia and anxiety. Panic attacks were a daily occurrence and my relationship with my partner was incredibly strained. It was the beginning of the pandemic, the world around us was imploding and our family and community were far away.

My daughter was tenacious and headstrong from birth. She was often unsettled and refused the breast for months, forcing me to exclusively pump before I softened and gratefully accepted the miracle of formula. As a new mother in lockdown I was forced to become extremely present and highly creative. Keeping a growing child entertained with no external stimulation is an excellent test of resourcefulness and aptitude as a parent. I was surprised to find that I loved the challenge of meeting my daughter's needs. Around the time of her first birthday my partner was still walking on eggshells around me in fear of my ever-present outbursts. I started working with a women's naturopath to balance my hormones and my moods.

It wasn't until I stopped breastfeeding, just shy of two years postpartum, that my moods and anxiety finally stabilised. By that time my partner and I had discussed at length whether there would ever be another child. Our initial hesitations, centring around my mental health and its impact on our family, were replaced by longer-term considerations as we settled into parenthood and the trauma of the pandemic began to fade. Both of us had always assumed there would be two, so it came as a surprise that our conversations always ended with a conclusion

that we felt we were simply happier people, and better parents, of an only child. We relish the relationship we have with our daughter and embrace the challenge of cultivating community, so that she will grow up with many close friends. We are in a good place. I have enough humility to accept that our minds may change, but my intuition tells me that our family size now will allow each of us to thrive for years to come.

Holly Norman, freelance creative and mother of Matilda

JULIET'S STORY

Within hours of Sol's birth, I said, 'Let's do it again!' He turns one next month and it was always my intention to try again when he turned one. Now here we are and I am ready to throw caution to the wind but we are also at a stage where things are full-on and it's hard to find balance and time for each other. My partner Nick doesn't think we should throw another baby into the mix but I think, why prolong it? It's chaos anyway. I long for another baby and I don't know how to stop that longing. Sometimes I think, *will I ever get to a point where I know that it will be my last baby?* I think I will but I don't know how that will feel.

Juliet Allen, sexologist and mother of Milli and Sol

Honouring

The honouring season of motherhood does not begin and end in the way seasons typically do. It is an ever-present state of being, a daily ritual, a deep breath in the midst of chaos, an understanding of the cultural context in which we find ourselves – that is, a world that does not acknowledge or value our deep, important and invisible work – and a letting go of the guilt that burden brings. Honouring your motherhood season is also about acknowledging and making space for your matrescence journey. This is a season rich with personal growth, identity and relationship shifts and radical changes in body and mind. There is beauty in all of this but there is also grief – a letting go of what was and moving forward into the unknown. Go gently. Society does not honour mothers so we must ensure we celebrate and respect ourselves and each other every minute, every hour, every day.

Motherhood, feminism and the patriarchy

I first learnt about the patriarchy as an eight-year-old sitting at my grandparents' dining room table, listening to my grandmother tell a story about when she refused to milk the cows one sunny Sunday in 1962.

My grandparents lived on a dairy farm in the Western District of Victoria. They had six children and on top of the endless cooking, cleaning, washing, scrubbing and mothering expected of her, my grandmother also milked their large herd of cows twice a day. Her days began at 4 am and ended around midnight. As a child, I never saw her without an apron on, and I remember she'd always sit with both legs to one side of her chair to be ready at a moment's notice to get something for someone. Once a year, my grandfather would take three weeks off to visit family in New Zealand on his own. My grandmother's yearly holiday was taking all six children to Geelong for a week to see her parents. On the weekends, my grandfather and the older children would pile into the car for a day at the local bike races – my uncle was a champion cyclist who went on to win a silver medal at the Olympics. It was never a discussion that my grandmother would be the one to stay home with the younger children and milk the cows.

On this particular weekend, when my grandfather got in the car, my grandmother was in the passenger seat.

'What are you doing?' he asked.

'I'm coming,' she said.

'But who will milk the cows?'

'I don't know,' she said. 'Who will?'

There was a bit more back and forth, she told me, but she held firm. From that day on, a farmhand was hired to milk the cows each weekend so my grandmother could go with her family to watch her son ride. Her small but mighty dissent echoed through my consciousness as a child and today when I think of that story, I love her even more for the courage and grit it took for her to take back a small piece of equality in an unequal life.

Today, nothing much has changed. As women and mothers, we continue to live in a state of economic, political, social and cultural oppression. The second wave of feminism in the sixties and seventies forged a path for us to step into the workplace, but it forgot that someone still had to show up at home – and so we did that as well. This wave of feminism was supposed to be about choice: to give us the freedom to choose to work outside the home or inside the home or both if we wanted. Women were conditioned to strive for 'having it all' when really all that ever meant was doing it all and becoming exhausted, depleted and angry in the process. What we need are cultural, political and workplace overhauls that recognise we have been taking on too much for too long. At the very least, we need to start placing value on work in the home and we need to normalise and make mandatory extended paid parental leave for both parents so families are supported to achieve greater equality from the beginning of a child's life.

Currently, if we choose to or have to go back to work after having a baby, we are met with a stark gender pay gap and childcare that is often expensive and sometimes more than we are earning. We are still managing the bulk of the caregiving and domestic load at home, all of which makes it challenging if not impossible to show up at work, gain positions of leadership and fight for institutional and political change. We simply don't have the time. And we're tired. And fed-up.

Mothers have been exhausted for millennia.

There is so much recovery work that needs to be done.

"

Patty Wipfler
Founder, Hand in Hand Parenting, a nonprofit
organisation that supports parents and families by nurturing
the parent–child connection, and mother of two sons

God forbid if we gave
motherhood value then our dirty
little secret would be exposed:
that our entire society is built
on the unpaid labour of women.
We tell women that the work they
are doing is caregiving, not labour.
One hundred per cent it is labour.
And it's unpaid. And without
women doing $1.9 trillion of
unpaid labour a year, our society
wouldn't function. So it's a benefit
of a patriarchal capitalist society
to devalue the thing that actually
has the most value in the world.

"

Eve Rodsky
Author, activist and mother of Zac, Ben and Anna

If we choose to stay home – and I acknowledge that is a privilege not afforded to all – our role is not valued, it's not paid, it's not acknowledged as work and we're judged for being 'just a mum'. If you're a mum who doesn't work outside of mothering, you'll be familiar with that awkward pause that happens when someone asks what you do for work and you tell them you're at home full-time. It's the most important job in the world, yet it carries no value because it doesn't contribute in an economic sense to our capitalist culture. Where's the output of holding your newborn as they sleep all day? Or stopping to watch the ants on your walk to the shops? Or wrangling three children out the door by 8 am? Or trying to dress a stubborn three-year-old? Or cooking, cleaning and shopping with a baby on your hip and a toddler at your feet? I can't think of anything in the world that has more value than parenting, but the value isn't measurable in the way our society likes to measure. It's simply expected of us and if it's 'all we do', we feel like we're letting our feminist sisters down. Our post-feminist-revolution generation grew up being asked, 'What are you going to do (outside of being a mum)?', as if being a mum is not enough on its own.

Regardless of the decisions we choose to or have to make, all women are put in the mother box the minute we have children. Our identity and worth are tied to our motherhood status in a way that just doesn't happen to men. We are judged and scrutinised and the expectations on us are so much greater, and this is where guilt seeps in. Women are expected to be with their children in a way that men are not. Men 'babysit', women mother. When we ask for more help at home, it's often perceived as nagging, when we shouldn't have to ask for help in the first place – the work of the home and raising children should never be the work of one person in a two-parent household. We have so far to go to break down these walls. I look at my daughters and my son and think about how it will be for them. What they witness at home are the patterns that will play out when they become parents and I hope we are showing them the way.

Our society and culture does not value the role of mother. Mothering is unpaid and we live in a capitalist, consumerist society where value equals dollars. When women say, 'I'm just a mother', it's reflecting the broader cultural value system we have internalised. Removing 'just' can be a revolutionary act in and of itself, but we receive pushback from that. We are asked, 'When are you going back to work?' Our identity is attached to the value we are perceived to offer the world and mothering is seen as not doing anything, it's seen as not contributing.

"

Dr Sophie Brock
Motherhood studies sociologist and mother of one

I wish all mothers knew that everything they are doing has value and that every type of family structure has value – whether you are a stay-at-home mum or a working mum. Whatever you contribute to the fabric of our society matters and you have been gaslit for too long into believing your contributions don't count.

"

Eve Rodsky
Author, activist and mother of Zac, Ben and Anna

I am a diehard feminist so what I am about to say is no criticism of the phenomenal changes that these women in history have made for us. But when we put women in the workplace and changed our role in society, we forgot motherhood. Feminism forgot motherhood. It devalued motherhood. We needed to break the idea that because you are a woman all you are here to do is get married and have babies – and it was an absolutely necessary step – but in the process we ignored the importance of being a mum. We grew up being asked, 'Who will you be, other than a mother?' And we are now in this place of trying to prove our value to the world because culturally, our value doesn't come from being a mum. It's really important for women to realise that their struggle with 'just' being a mum is tied to the economic value of what we do. If we paid women for it, motherhood would be valued.

"

Amy Taylor-Kabbaz
Author, journalist, matrescence activist
and mother of Scarlett, Greta and Cassius

Researching for this book I came across the term matricentric feminism for the first time, initially in conversation with author, journalist and matrescence activist Amy Taylor-Kabbaz and then in more depth during my interview with Professor Andrea O'Reilly. Matricentric feminism is feminism that puts the mother's needs and concerns at the centre. The term was coined by O'Reilly when she became a mother and realised that there was very little representation for mothers in the theory and practice of feminism. It's fascinating to go deep into this work and unpack the history of feminism and how motherhood was devalued and even demonised over time. It was seen as the patriarchal trap, that when you became a mother you went to the other side and could no longer be a feminist. In her incredible volume of work, O'Reilly argues that the opposite is true, that motherhood galvanises women, that when women become mothers they become so enraged, they find feminism. Her work has become a portal to social, cultural and political change with empowerment of mothers at the centre. It has personally helped me feel seen and understood and acknowledged for all the feelings I have ever felt since becoming a mother. Take a look at her work, and I promise you'll feel validated, less alone and empowered to shift what is not serving you.

ANDREA'S STORY

In the early eighties, I was doing a BA in Women's Studies and English. The last thing I was thinking about was motherhood. Then I became unexpectedly pregnant at twenty-two and realised just how invisible motherhood was in all the courses I was taking. I was in my third year and it was rarely mentioned, and when it was spoken about it was in a very negative way. I was outraged and inspired. I got pregnant again, and then again – I had three children in five years while doing my BA, my MA, and then my PhD. Around that time I was teaching a course called 'Introduction to feminism'. We studied liberal feminism, socialist feminism, radical cultural feminism, womanism, eco feminism, third wave feminism, political feminism – but guess what? None of them focused on mothers. I thought, if we could have all these feminisms that represent and speak to a particular group (young women, poor women, racialised women, global women), we also needed a feminism that began with and centred on the needs and concerns of mothers. In my research and conversations with women, I have found that motherhood matters more than gender in terms of their oppression. Having a child changes women and creates new priorities and new problems. We needed a feminism that asked women: what do you need to challenge oppressions? To be empowered as a mother? And so I developed a course dedicated to motherhood and coined the term matricentric feminism, a feminism that put mothers at the centre.

I do this work to create a space for motherhood and to give it legitimacy and visibility because in our culture it is invisible, taken for granted, and not seen as work. Our culture expects women to do it out of love and purports it to be all instinct and intuition. But, no, motherhood is work and our culture would fall apart in a second if women withdrew that labour. We have to recognise it as such and support it. We need partners to step up. We need policy shifts that make parental leave compulsory for men. We need national childcare programs that are affordable. And we need to listen to mothers and share our stories to find support and validation for all we are doing.

Andrea O'Reilly, PhD, full professor in the School of Gender, Sexuality and Women's Studies at York University, founder and director of The Motherhood Initiative (1998–2019), founder of the *Journal of the Motherhood Initiative,* editor/author of twenty-five books, publisher of Demeter Press and mother of three

When I first had a baby, I came to the realisation that motherhood is not respected or honoured or valued. I was home and I didn't know how to be home. I didn't know how to value home. When women left the home to go into the working world, we all pretended like the feminine realm was not important. The truth is, everybody needs a warm home – but this work is not respected, it's not honoured and there is no payment for it, which is how value is given in our society. We are in deep repair of patriarchal systems and are only just beginning to understand that the home has value and that home energy is vital for the health of every person and every family. The realm of the feminine is the work of our time.

"

Tami Lynn Kent
Author of *Wild Creative*, *Wild Feminine* and *Mothering From Your Center*, and mother of three sons

My girl, you'll need
to speak louder

'I want to hold him,' she said,
As they whisked her son away
Forced to stay in the hospital room,
With no goodbyes to her babe

She went home,
Her arms empty, her heart weak
And no answers on why he was gone,
No space for her to ask or to speak

It was 1948
And her voice had no power
So she said to her daughter
'My girl, you'll need to speak louder'

She suffered in silence,
Through her raw postpartum haze
Asking for help was not an option
Because the home was her duty, always

So she carried the load,
She carried it all
And she held her head high,
There was no room to fall

It was 1986
And her voice had little power
So she said to her daughter,
'My girl, you'll need to speak louder'

I pleaded to the doctor,
These symptoms won't go away
'It's just your period,' he said
'Every woman feels that pain'

But I went back again,
'Listen to me,' I demanded
Still, two decades it took to be heard,
And for a cause to be found

It was 2022
And my voice was slowly gaining power
Still, I said to my daughter,
'My girl, you'll need to speak louder'

I'm so sorry,
You still have to fight to be heard
I'm so sorry,
Politicians remove your rights with
Their words
I'm so sorry,
You won't be paid equal to your brother
I'm so sorry,
You'll still carry the mental load,
Not your partner
I'm so sorry,
The patriarchy will be everywhere
You roam
And I'm sorry,
You can't feel safe walking home

For now, my strong girl,
I'll speak for you, as your mama
I'll fight for your rights
I'll fight like no other

And one day I'll tell you,
Speak louder, shout and shout again
Don't stop until the world hears
Raise your fist, dissent

Speak until your voice holds
Boundless power,
And an equal future is all that you see
Until you can finally tell your daughter,
'My girl, just be'

Justine Hughes, mother of Edie

The mental, emotional, invisible load

You know that endless list of family admin, stress and worry that ping-pongs around your head at all times – book the appointment, plan the party, finish the forms, must get nappies, pack the bags, find that missing sock, worry about the lingering cough, wash the sheets, meet the teacher, plan the meals, buy the food? It's called the mental and emotional load and all current research points to the fact that women overwhelmingly take on the bulk of it in heterosexual relationships.

This isn't the narrative for all families, but for a lot of women – I'd argue most – it begins when our children are born and we take more time off than our partners and inevitably start taking on more because we're the ones at home. Then we go back to work and continue doing it all because it has become invisible. Then we feel like we're nagging if we ask for help and sometimes when we do ask it doesn't get done or it's not done well and so it falls back on us and the cycle goes on.

I remember James coming home one Friday night after what had been a particularly rough day for me – pre-pandemic when he'd leave the house early and get home late five days a week. Our girls were four and one, it was winter, the days were long and cold and wet and I had no idea what to cook for dinner. He came in through our back gate and casually removed his

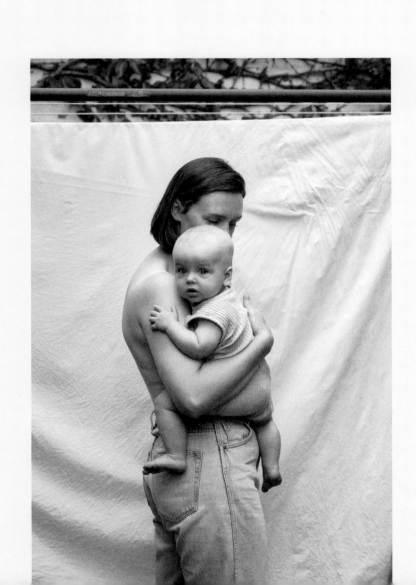

earphones after what I imagined was a leisurely commute home listening to a podcast and zoning out and I absolutely lost it. Lost it. I was so angry at him for having time every morning and every night on his way to and from work all to himself, to listen to whatever he wanted, to have that mental and physical space that I craved. It had been so long since I'd had even a minute to myself to do anything. He didn't deserve all my anger. I didn't recognise it at the time, but it was really aimed at our patriarchal society that has expected mothers to suck it up for so long, and devalues our role and demands we keep this never-ending and invisible to-do list and hold our families together while having very little support or time for ourselves.

It's going to take time for the walls of the patriarchy to come down and to ensure that happens, change has to come from within our homes. We have to have conversations with our partners about what is not serving us, about what we need to let go of and what we need them to take on. We have to name and divide the labour. We need to fight for equal parental leave and both parents need to take it. We need to start seeing our time as equally valuable to that of our partner's – even if we don't work as much or earn less or have more flexible jobs, as Eve Rodsky argues so well in her phenomenal book *Fair Play* (essential reading for all families). We need to acknowledge as a couple that both parents need time alone to do whatever they need to do to come back to themselves – and we need to schedule that into the week and ensure space is made so we can follow through. We cannot have one partner thinking only of themselves until they are asked to do something for the family. It's not our job to be caring for our children and the home 24/7 to the point that we are forced to ask for help when we need it – our partner needs to anticipate and recognise the needs of our children and the family and the home. We have been conditioned into believing that the invisible load of motherhood is an expectation that falls solely on our shoulders, that it is caregiving, that it is what a 'good mother' does.

Actually, it's the hardest job in the world and should be recognised as such, and partners need to step up and workplaces and governments need to make space for them to be at home so they can witness the work and understand what has to be done – to see what we have been doing for so long.

The Motherhood Space

It's not as easy as just telling a mother to lower her expectations, to step back and do less, because we face consequences for that. When we step back and do less, who is the one stepping in to do more? We can't shift the mental load until we make it visible, name it, and look at the redistribution of labour in the domestic realm.

"

Dr Sophie Brock
Motherhood studies sociologist and mother of one

Men have been taught since they were born that their time is diamonds and we've been taught that our time is sand. When our kids are home sick from school we cancel our day to stay home with them because we see our time as less valuable, or our jobs as more flexible, or maybe we don't make as much money as our partner. Equality in the home is about having control over how we spend our time. If we are the ones who are always expected to cancel our day, we don't have time choice over that day and that's not fair. All time is created equal, no matter how much money we make or how flexible our jobs are and when we start to push back on the notion that our time is less valuable, men start doing more and society starts to change. We shouldn't be asking men to be less selfish with their time. We should learn to be more selfish with ours.

"

Eve Rodsky
Author, activist and mother of Zac, Ben and Anna

Let me put a paradigm out there. The patriarchy is alive and well and it trickles down. Because members of the patriarchy make more money, their work is seen as more valuable than the work that is done in the home. Mothering is largely invisible. That's really problematic because it plays out in a power differential in couples. We need to talk about this, we need to name it and we need to fight the problem together rather than fighting each other. We are not the problem, the society we live in is the problem. The system sets us up to fail and while it's not the partner's fault, it doesn't mean they can't do something about it.

"

Kara Hoppe
Psychotherapist, author, teacher and
mother of Jude and Dione

Some mothers I spoke to for this book shared that they carried the emotional load for their family – the worrying, the holding space, the holding hands – because they felt they were better at it and biologically more wired to do it. But I don't subscribe to this and neither did the experts I spoke to. I do think that culturally men have not been expected to do this more emotional caregiving work – nor have they been raised to do it – so women have taken it on as yet another thing, but that doesn't mean that can't and shouldn't change. I believe men are equally capable of doing this work and doing it well and I've witnessed it. Make a decision as a family for your partner to take as much parental leave as possible and then give them space to step into this role and share this important work. Our children don't learn by what we tell them, they learn by what they see. Having fathers gently support the emotional needs of their children can do so much for healing their own childhood wounds of not being seen and met in the way they needed to be emotionally, and also paves the way for boys to become fathers who feel at home in a nurturing role, and that can only be a very good thing.

I think that we do a disservice
to men by presuming they don't
have the capacity to engage in
emotional labour. All mothers
know that parenting is not just
intuitive: we don't always know
what we are doing and we are
constantly learning and practising.
Fathers need time with their
children to find their feet too, but
we don't have a system, structure
or workplaces that enable and
support them to do so.

"

Dr Sophie Brock
Motherhood studies sociologist and mother of one

Mother rage is an accumulation of stress. We are not getting our needs met: we haven't had enough sleep, we haven't eaten, we are touched out, we need more support, there is a negative loop that is spiralling in our minds and there's an accumulation of old traumas and wounds that get activated when we become mothers because we are stepping into a role where we are mostly powerless. We grew up being good girls. We weren't allowed to express our anger and our rage and our frustration. We had to repress it and find ways to numb it. The message we got was: don't be hysterical, don't be crazy, don't be dramatic. Then we become mothers and experience this powerlessness all the time and what happens is it taps us back into all those powerless feelings we had when we were little. When we lean into that, there is a lot of pain and hurt. Because when we become parents and if we are trying to do it consciously, we look at our own childhoods and realise, I was not met in the way I needed to be. There is a lot of repressed pain there that we don't allow ourselves to feel.

"

Lael Stone
Speaker, author, educator, creator and
mother of Ky, Indi and Tali

Motherhood rage

Today, there is a growing mainstream body of work examining motherhood rage, an emotion that was once taboo.

When I was a new mother, I'd never come across the term, never seen 'motherhood' and 'rage' in the same sentence. So, when I felt it coming up from deep within – a sharp, explosive anger – I was ashamed and scared. What was this?

A few years ago, I discovered Molly Caro May's book *Body Full of Stars* and it changed my life. The subhead on the cover reads, 'Female rage and my passage into motherhood' – which felt revolutionary to me. Another mother understands what I am going through! And she's putting it out there for the world to read! I related to so much of what she wrote, and I asked James to read it too so he'd know that I'm not the only one who explodes.

Of course we experience rage as women and mothers. Of course we are angry. For all the reasons I have examined in this book, and a thousand more. We have inherited the trauma and grief of our mothers and grandmothers – the burdens, the expectations, the silent suffering, the unmet needs and unrealised dreams – and we carry it all alongside our own. We are overwhelmed, we are depleted, and we are very, very tired. We lack support, value, validation, equality, community, food and rest. We are paid less for the same job. In many countries our bodily autonomy has been taken away. We are disrespected and violated. We are not safe walking home. In Australia, one woman a week is murdered by her current or former partner. The World Health Organization estimates one in three women globally has been abused physically and/or sexually in their lifetime. I am angry as a white middle-class woman who feels safe at home and has all the privilege in the world, so I can only begin to imagine the depths of anger and despair felt by women of colour, women living in poverty, women living in fear and women who can't access safe abortion. And it cannot be overlooked that some mothers –

particularly Indigenous mothers and women of colour – have valid fears that if they express their anger and rage then they are at far greater risk of losing their children than a white woman is, so when we talk about motherhood rage we must also consider who has licence and feels safe enough to speak their truth – certainly not all women.

The rage isn't going anywhere and it cannot be diffused with yoga and self-care. We need safe spaces to let it out and we need to recognise the oppression of women and mothers and do something about it on a micro and a macro level. And while society takes its time to sort all this out, don't feel guilty when you feel the rage rising. It's not your fault. It was never your fault.

The antidote to the anger and rage we experience as mothers is a safe place to share exactly how we are feeling without judgement. It's a toxic thing to try to get women to move through their anger quickly, to let them cry for five minutes and then say, 'Okay, now what are we going to do about this? Do you think if you got up earlier or maybe did a bit more self-care or have you tried this type of patting to get your baby to sleep?' She's not looking for answers. She needs to be heard.

"

Amy Taylor-Kabbaz
Author, journalist, matrescence activist
and mother of Scarlett, Greta and Cassius

Matrescence is a transformation from who
we used to be to the woman we are going
to become. But the middle part is so painful.
It is confronting, lonely, and dark. It can also
be filled with spectacular awakenings but
I think the reason we find it so challenging is
because we don't know that it's normal to feel
this way and we don't know how to let go of
that part of ourselves that isn't there anymore.
We are not going to show up to our work the
way we used to, we are not going to show up in
our relationships the way we used to, everything
has changed. And because we don't talk about
it in our culture, this inner-split we all feel as
we move into motherhood stays with us and
it gets bigger and harder and more painful. It's
why so many women I work with, when I explain
this inner-split to them, there is a realisation
of, 'Ahhhhhh, that's why I feel the way I do.'

"

Amy Taylor-Kabbaz
Author, journalist, matrescence activist
and mother of Scarlett, Greta and Cassius

Matrescence and identity

When a child becomes an adult they have a period of messy transition we call adolescence. They don't know who they are, they question everything and they experience a complete hormonal, physical, spiritual shift that is accepted, understood and revered in our culture.

Matrescence, or the transition to motherhood, is less understood and rarely acknowledged, which makes it even more challenging and painful for women moving through it. Society wants us to be happy all the time: glowing, thankful, in awe of our baby and this new life. And we are happy, but it's also really hard. It's normal and human to question what we have done and to miss our old life. There's competition and comparison and the weight of the 'good mother' narrative and we attach ourselves to that identity and measure ourselves against it. We experience ambivalence, isolation, boredom, loneliness, rage, fear, anxiety and grief. There is a deep knowing that we are losing parts of ourselves and we're not yet sure who will emerge. It is a huge shift between two worlds. We have to learn to navigate all this, to stand in the fire and surrender, but most of us haven't been shown the way – we're not surrounded by elders who normalise the transition and remind us that it takes years and years to unfold, and with each new baby we are reborn as a mother and a new transition begins.

As we move through matrescence, it's so important to take up space with our stories. There is science behind the shifts we experience during this season – chemical changes in our brain matter, psychological awakenings, hormonal surges – but there is also so much that science can't explain and storytelling is the answer. We need to share the truth about this time

I miss the maiden.
I miss her freedom, her
naivety, her spontaneity,
her energy. But I don't
look back with envy.

"

Kate Bloom
Birth and postpartum doula and
mother of Jozie, Pixie and Dustyn

and how hard it can be. We need a safe space to share what we're going through – the joy and the pain. I promise you, whatever you are feeling, no matter how dark, another mother has felt it before you. By acknowledging and honouring this shift, you are also healing the intergenerational trauma of our mothers and grandmothers who weren't given the space to slowly emerge anew and who were expected to take their place in the home without question and with so much sacrifice. We naturally carry their unspoken struggles into our own motherhood journey and by honouring our transition and giving ourselves grace and time we are also healing their stories and paving the way for our daughters to fully come into their journey of motherhood with reverence.

Motherhood has changed me in so many ways and I am only just beginning to understand all that has shifted and continues to shift for me. In the beginning, for those first couple of years, I was too deep in it to acknowledge the magnitude of what was happening – the slow yet complete unravelling of self. I had a sense that my priorities had changed and the things I cared so much about before no longer felt so important to me. I watched as relationships ended and others started anew and there was grief and beauty in that. I missed and mourned parts of my old life – the spontaneity, the freedom, the sleep-ins, the long showers, the late dinners, the time alone, the clear head – and I found peace in places where I least expected to. I reassessed my career and walked away from a job and a city I loved, to spend more time with Camille, which, in the end, was the easiest hard decision I have ever had to make. I loved being at home with her and even though I was met with too many 'oh, so you're just a mother?' and 'I could never do that, I need to use my brain' comments slipped in mid-conversation, I feel lucky to have had this time – the slow days felt sacred to me, having not been as present as I would have liked for her first year of life. Even so, after I left my job, I did wrestle with the decision and wonder if I'd done the right thing leaving behind all the praise and acknowledgement and status and value and money that came with a role I'd worked so hard for. And the passing comments about me 'just' being a mother did make me stop and think, am I doing enough? But for the year I stayed home with my daughter, I allowed myself to sink in and feel it all. I'll be forever grateful for that time and the peace it brought to both our lives.

Eventually, I started to think about my career again. Of course I did. Like all women of my generation, I had absorbed the message that I should be able to balance motherhood and a paid job – as if the one I was doing 24/7 at home wasn't enough. And I did miss paid work. I wanted a career. I just wasn't sure what paid work I wanted to do anymore. I wasn't sure who I was anymore. I was in the very privileged position to be able to ask: *What job would make being away from my daughter worthwhile?* I ended up accepting a part-time consulting role at a female-run company when Camille was two. There I watched brilliant women return from maternity leave and be cast aside and overlooked. I too was in line for a leadership role, an opportunity that was promptly taken away the minute they learnt I was pregnant for the second time. It struck me then and I still see it everywhere today: there is such little respect for mothers in the workplace. How are those of us who choose to work outside of the home supposed to find our feet amidst this radical transformation when we are given such little support to excel in the roles we love and are very good at, and that matter so much to us? And as a society, how much talent are we missing out on by not supporting mothers in their return to work with equal opportunity, equal pay, respect and acknowledgement?

I left that consulting job after Audrey was born and haven't worked in an office since. Sometimes I'm jealous of James's work trips and dinners that go late into the night and I wish I had colleagues to hang out with, a work life outside of our home. My paid work today is varied and I wear many hats: doula, author, educator, small business owner. I exist in the push and the pull. I love my career, and I love to be home – and because I mostly work from home the lines often blur. When I do leave the house for work, Camille, Audrey and Freddie stand shoulder to shoulder at our window, noses pressed up to the glass waving goodbye with both hands. I always think, how can I possibly leave these beautiful creatures? And yet I love to be on my own, to have the space and time to think and work and create. The push and the pull.

Every day since Camille's birth, motherhood has held a mirror up to my life that, when I finally felt ready to look into it, helped bring into focus what mattered and what was no longer serving me. I left my corporate career to become a doula and open a business that has community at its heart. I wrote my first book and this is my second. For the first time in my life, I feel my work honours who I am, and I never would have found this path had I not become a mother. It has been my greatest transformation.

The Motherhood Space

For many years I thought I stepped away from my career because I couldn't cope. Because I couldn't be the journalist I wanted to be and the mum I wanted to be so I had to make a choice. In feminist literature it is called the perceived choice: we are told we have a choice but we actually don't. Because we can't work the way they are asking us to and be the mother we want to be. If we understood matrescence in the workplace better I think we would be able to keep more women in the roles that they love.

"

Amy Taylor-Kabbaz
Author, journalist, matrescence activist
and mother of Scarlett, Greta and Cassius

Motherhood and birth unravelled me, expanded me, and turned me into who I came to be – a mother and as a teacher. Motherhood showed me what I'm capable of and what's important to fight for.

"

Jane Hardwicke Collings
Women's mysteries teacher, shamanic craftswoman, midwife, writer, teacher, mother and grandmother

YEONG'S STORY

It starts simple enough. One day you decide (or your body decides) you're going to be a mother. And so it begins: the journey into pregnancy, birth, babies and beyond. You think you have some idea of what it's going to be like – there are so many mothers out there, after all. And then, your baby arrives. Breaks your heart, body and mind open to reveal a whole side of life you've never experienced. It's joyful and exhilarating, but also so, so exhausting. The hormones, the constant wake-ups, the second guessing of every decision. Relentless. No two babies are the same, which makes it even harder to decipher which advice or opinion you'll ultimately take on. Often you try everything, falling down 3 am rabbit holes of Reddit threads and parenting forums in the search for answers. You ask strangers, friends, relatives what worked for them. And all the while, as you're doing everything to keep this precious little human alive, you notice yourself change.

First, it's your body. Pregnancy isn't always kind. Stretch marks, loose skin and pigmentation. New lines appear on your face, and if you're one of the lucky few, your hair may even sprout its first greys like mine did during my second pregnancy. Birth? Well, that's another story altogether. But as the saying goes: these things too shall pass, and like everything else in life, soften and become acceptable with time. Besides, beyond the physical aspect, the most dramatic imprint of motherhood lies in your sense of self. It is both easy and commonplace to lose yourself in the humdrum moments and repetitive nature of child rearing. You will find yourself doing things you'd previously never dreamt of, like giving up sushi, cheese, ice-cream and hot chips in the quest to relieve your baby's silent reflux (anything for a better night's sleep!). One day, you'll realise you know all the words to 'Let It Go' and catch yourself humming Wiggles nursery rhymes, even when your child is at daycare. You'll start saying things that make you sound unmistakably old: 'Careful!', 'Watch your head!', 'Hold my hand!' Nothing makes you age faster than becoming a parent.

But here's the thing about motherhood: it may alter your mind, your body and your soul permanently, but in crossing that threshold, you don't fully forget who you were. You may wave goodbye to Sunday morning lie-ins, 9 pm dinner bookings and last-minute trips away, but the pre-kid ghost still lingers. Even if you accept the pub being replaced by playgrounds, and master the art of cramming a shower, Pilates workout and laundry load into a single forty-five-minute sleep cycle, there are still times you'll glance in the mirror – through tears and bloodshot eyes – and

The Motherhood Space

simply not recognise yourself. 'What is my life?', you'll say, and it's true, it won't look like it used to. You'll see old memories pop up on your phone and marvel at your easy holidays, thriving social life and well-rested visage. Instead, your house will be permanently bomb-struck, dishes and laundry will pile up faster than you can say, 'Where's the remote?' And your once sharp mind and reliable memory? Well, let's just say they've taken a leave of absence.

Truth is, you might not ever get your clean house and easy existence back – not least until the kids have left the nest. You may also come to the startling conclusion that working nine to five and caring for children don't exactly align. (Society, it seems, doesn't always reward ambitious mothers, and besides, parenting is the hardest job you'll ever have.) Your career might take a back seat to just muddling through the work week, and the simplest of social activities will suddenly require a Herculean organisational effort and weeks of planning. But actually, it's okay. Over time, you realise you wouldn't want everything to stay the same forever. Jobs come and go. You won't always live in activewear. To stand still is to be stagnant, and life doesn't work that way. Having children, you'll soon realise, shows you just how quickly time passes. It is both the blessing and curse of parenthood; you can't choose what to pause and what to fast forward. Newborn cuddles don't last, but thankfully neither do sleep regressions, tantrums and teething. You can rail against your toddler waking you at 1 am to wipe off a droplet of milk from her face (true story), but you can also love her so fiercely, you won't feel complete without her in your arms. And never, ever discount how easily a simple laugh or gummy smile can melt you, even at your darkest, most emotionally spent hour.

Then there's all the things motherhood brings into sharp focus. Not the things you expect, mind you. Sure, you get a kick out of seeing the same-coloured eyes staring back at you and the sight of your child's tiny hands and feet (miniatures of yours) resting next to you, but it's more than that. You see snippets of your own personality – both good and bad – coming out. You laugh and spar with your partner about which traits you're responsible for, but soon realise having children is far less a narcissistic urge to replicate your own genes, and more a chance to time travel back to your own childhood. Fact is, you adore them, not because they came from you, but simply because of the miracle of their existence. There's no bigger privilege or responsibility than nurturing a human from birth until adulthood, and while the sacrifices are many, the rewards are sweet. And any time you think you've lost complete sight of yourself, remember that the sleep deprivation and the chaos won't last. Just like they won't be small enough to nurse in your arms forever, one day, they'll be mature enough to venture into the world independently, and the blessing will be knowing you've done your job just right.

Yeong Sassall, digital editor and mother of Camille and Ollie

It's okay not to know how to do this. And it's okay not to know how to feel about that. It's okay to miss your old life. It's okay to want to go back to work, or to not want to go back to work. Nobody knows how motherhood is going to impact them until they are a mother. Everyone responds to it differently, and it's always changing. It's very fluid. Extend yourself as much grace as possible. It's really difficult, especially in the beginning.

"

Kara Hoppe
Psychotherapist, author, teacher and
mother of Jude and Dion

SARAH'S STORY

In my early postpartum days, I teetered between two emotional poles: a consuming rush of love for my baby, and my terrible struggle with breastfeeding.

A while later, when my husband went back to work, the interstate visitors returned home and the house grew quiet, an unfamiliar feeling crept in. My baby would only sleep on me and I spent hours pinned beneath her. It was there that I was slowly overwhelmed by the crushing sensation that my life had changed beyond recognition and my time was no longer my own.

Rather than longing for fancy dinners and dance floors, I mourned the days when I had the freedom to choose when to go to the bathroom or get a drink of water. Every second of my time was devoted to my baby's presence. I spent my 'alone time' dreading the relentless cycle of breastfeeding, soothing and tending to which I knew I must soon return. I cried often. Soon, these sensations culminated into a feeling that I had experienced before: grief.

My old self, I believed, had died.

I loved my baby and knew no greater joy than her. Yet beneath this sea of happiness ran a cold and lonely current of mourning. I had always known that having a baby would change my existence beyond recognition, but I hadn't expected to lose myself completely. Looking back, I was too deep in the fog of the fourth trimester to understand that it wouldn't always be this way.

My baby is now one. When I think back on that transformative, exhausting period, I still feel a sense of sadness and sorrow for that girl. Dirty hair and milk-stained clothes, her nipples raw and aching sitting on bruised and swollen skin, with a mind that struggled through broken sleep. I believe that my grief was as real and valid as the life-changing, soul-igniting love that I felt for my child. It took me a long time to understand that both of those emotions could be felt concurrently.

Slowly, I realised that the 'old me' had not died. She reappeared. Transformed, changed irrevocably for the better – but still me.

I had resurfaced.

The Motherhood Space

Resurfaced

I once believed
That the old me had died,
That the girl I had been before
Must have bled from my body
When my baby was born,
Lost among the fluids
On the birthing unit floor,
Her remains to be cremated,
An independence destined
For the hospital incinerator.

And I mourned her passing
As I would an old friend.
How could I continue blindly,
Navigate this unfamiliar territory
When my guide was gone?
For all that I had known about myself
Seemed lost, irrelevant,
Redundant in this place;
The life I had lived
Dismantled in an instant
By the life that I held in my arms.

And there in that limbo
I gave all of me,
Every spark of my energy,
Every moment of night and day.
And I wept as I gazed
Upon the sweet beauty I had made –
For I knew no greater love or joy –
Yet whenever I saw myself,
I turned away
From the pale reflection
That I was not ready to face.

I can still see that version of me.
A mother who had given everything
For the angel in her arms,
Driving the girl she had been
To a place dark and deeply inward,
Where she waited,
Coiled, cocooned,
Yet still alive.

If only I could have told myself
This period is temporary.
If only I could have held her,
Wiped tears and promised her
That her time would return to her,
Slowly, a little more each month.
That the pale reflection would change,
That life would return to that face,
A life she recognised.

For one day –
Shifted,
Expanded,
Shining with new facets
Hewn from the pressure,
Transformed forever,
Yet still a part of me
That I had longed for and remembered
– she had not died.
She rose, returning from the depths,
And finally resurfaced.

Sarah Sky, writer and mother of one

You are enough. We are living in a society and in a culture that is constantly telling us to do more, be more, have more. But we can release so much pressure and uncover our own power by recognising we are already enough and we are doing the best we can in the context in which we find ourselves.

"

Dr Sophie Brock
Motherhood studies sociologist and mother of one

Be in circles of
women who see
and value your
experience of
motherhood
because that will
change your life.

"

Julie Tenner
Intimacy and relationship coach, doula and
mother of Heath, Jade, Lola and Gwen

Friendships and community

You know when you see another mother in the street and she's rocking her baby in the stroller or the carrier just the way you do, trying to get them to sleep, and for a moment you see yourself in her and smile because it brings you comfort? Motherhood is full of moments like that.

Each season – newborn, baby, toddler, schoolchildren, teenagers – brings with it a million unique challenges and relatable moments and finding a tribe to ride those waves alongside you is everything. There is solidarity and honesty in the friendships you make with other mothers in this season of your life. These relationships are life-saving and important, but not always that easy to come by. It's actually one of the most common questions the women I support in my doula work ask of me: where can I connect with other mothers?

Building your community takes time and will look different for everyone. You may be lucky enough to go through pregnancy with your best friend or sister, or you could be the first in your friendship group to have a baby and in that case there's often a period of postpartum mourning as you watch some of those friendships drop away for a while, sometimes forever. You might meet lifelong friends in your mothers' group or the library or in line for your morning coffee. I have met some of my best mum friends at the park because it always feels so natural to start a conversation there while our children play underfoot and we have time to talk and connect with coffee and fresh air.

I encourage you to be open and vulnerable as you gather your village. Community is all around us, but sometimes you have to be brave to uncover it. After my daughters' swimming lessons recently a mother asked if she could borrow our shampoo, apologising for not being more organised. I have been that mother before – we have all been that mother before – and I thanked her for asking me for help. No matter how big or small the favour, it's not easy to reach out. But your community of mothers is around you and there for you. Never apologise for asking for help or support or shampoo or wipes at the park. Be patient and put yourself out there and your tribe will find you, and when it does it is the most spectacular thing – to have found women who will be there for you in good times and bad. Friends who understand, who you don't have to explain yourself to, who you can sit comfortably in silence with and who with just one look know instantly how your day is going and how much sleep you got last night. That is one of the best things about motherhood: finding your people and knowing it will all be okay with them by your side.

One of the most significant lessons I learnt in the research and writing of this book came through conversations with Patty Wipfler, who is the founder of Hand in Hand Parenting, a nonprofit organisation that supports parents and families by nurturing the parent–child connection, and Lael Stone, who is a speaker, author and educator in the trauma and emotional awareness space. Both women spoke passionately about the need for all mothers to have a listening partner. A listening partner is your safe place, they are the person you call or text when you need to yell or scream or cry or rage. The listening partner is not there to offer solutions to your problems. They are simply there to listen. And you, in return, listen to them. They don't need special training and they don't need to be in the same season of life that you are. They could be your sister or a friend or a colleague or an elder. Someone you feel safe with and who you know will not bring judgement or their own stories to your narrative. When I heard Patty and Lael speak about this, it made so much sense: we cannot ignore our anger and hope it goes away. We need our emotions to be received, held and acknowledged, not judged or twisted. Find a listening partner and be a good listener yourself and your motherhood journey will be lighter for it.

We are not good at listening as humans. When someone is telling us about something, we are working out how to fix it in our head. We say, 'Oh I know how that feels!' and jump into their drama with them. The art of listening is to say, 'Oof, I hear you and I see you and I am sitting in this space with you and I trust you will find your way out of this.' A listening partner is there to bring this beautiful container of compassion to the hurt you are feeling. You get on the phone, swear your head off, rant and rave for twenty minutes, and the other person simply says, 'I hear you, you are doing an amazing job.'

"

Lael Stone
Speaker, author, educator, creator and
mother of Ky, Indi and Tali

I knew friendships were likely to shift but I don't think I anticipated how much or how sad it would make me. I am the first of my close friends to have a baby and this has been challenging. So much of motherhood can't be explained, even to the kindest, most supportive people in your life. Sometimes when spending time with friends, I feel like I am on the outside looking in at my old self and this can feel hard and strange. Perhaps most crushing is the lack of support from people you thought you could lean on. But just as motherhood has caused some friendships to drift, it has also gifted me incredible new connections. The shared experiences of parenting, in my experience, make it easy to open up conversation and pursue friendships with other women and this is something I love and embrace about motherhood.

"

Beth Ryan
Midwife and mother of Poppy

One more thing, before I close out this chapter. Every mother is walking her own journey and if I had one wish, it would be for us all to be at peace with our choices – to not feel the need to defend them and to celebrate and support the choices of others even if they are very different from our own. We are judged as mothers by society every day for the things we do and the things we don't do. We are judged for how we birth our babies, for how little or how long and even where we breastfeed our babies, for choosing to work outside the home or not work outside the home, for sleep training, for co-sleeping, for looking at our phone while at the park, for not loving mothering enough or for loving it too much. There's shame and judgement everywhere we go, so let's support each other. Remember that her choices and experiences are not an attack on yours. It's not a competition, this motherhood game.

The most important thing a mother can do is find her village. This is not as elusive as it at first seems. It may involve a hard edit of people in your life that you deeply care about. But it will also open up the path for people who are truly deserving to honour you and you in turn to honour them. Who will bring you your favourite nourishing meal in the tender first days? Who will respect your boundaries? Who will listen to you without judgement? Who makes you feel energised after spending time with them? These are your people. Spend time perfecting how to ask for what you need, and the art of receiving it too. Nothing fills an empty cup like giving, so don't forget to pay it forward when the time comes. As you shift and evolve in your new life, you may find your relationships shifting and evolving too. Leave space for this to happen, gracefully.

"

Justina Edwards
Mother of Sage and Dahlia

ROSE'S STORY

I drove my daughter to school recently, and on the way back saw Lisa, a friend, colleague and creative, leaving her house late for the drop-off. One kid was screaming, the other eating breakfast in the stroller. I knew she was solo parenting that week, with project deadlines she had to meet as well.

Before she got back, I went to her house, walked around to the back door, stepped over the pancakes on the floor, and popped a pot of minestrone in her fridge. I always make extra now, just in case.

She was so grateful. And said to me later during a morning walk around the village, 'Rose, not long ago I would have felt a lot of shame around you coming into my totally disordered house and seeing how out of control things were.'

I think a lot of mothers feel that shame about not having it together perfectly, not 'coping', not managing the juggle – a shame that cuts us off from receiving the care that we need.

I work in the postpartum space, and it's something I get asked a lot. How do I make a community? How do I feel less alone? How do I find friends as a new mother? I have my own version of those questions. How do we show up better for each other? How do we reduce social isolation?

Perhaps by looking at that shame piece, we can unlock the path for many of us to work towards finding the community that we not only long for, but biologically require, for us to thrive in our mothering and our aspirations.

The trust Lisa and I have developed over time has been the result of a lot of small steps towards each other. Our comfort with each other has taken faith and vulnerability, something I consider an investment in how I mother and how I live. It's so nice to be at the stage now where there is no hiding from each other.

I see how her professional life sits up nice and close to her mothering life, and it gives me inspiration to see how it can work, as a constantly evolving process that adapts as her children change and grow.

I see how she resources herself, the boundaries she uses, what gets prioritised; how she works through hard feelings, too. I know what is sacrificed, the tools they use as a family, their routines and flexibility, their values.

The Motherhood Space

I learn a lot from seeing how it works, up close to the beautiful mess of it all. The pancakes on the floor showed me not the chaos of Lisa's life, but the way she had prioritised fun and play with her girls that morning. Standing in the kitchen, I could still feel the joy in the room.

Conversations about the cultural visibility of motherhood tend to focus on the need for storytelling: more films, podcasts and novels sharing the honest experience of mothering in the modern world. These things can be such game changers for us all.

But more and more, I want to recognise the importance of being visible to each other. We need to invite each other into the beautiful chaos of our lives, and share without shame the way we juggle our dreams alongside our care work, to make money, to make our mark, and to inspire and nurture our kids.

I see others doing it online, something that kept me going during the pandemic. Each of us is finding a way. We are making choices unique to our generation, aligned with our values as modern women and as devoted mothers. And each of us shines a path for the next woman, and on it goes.

I'm inspired by projects like the Artist Residency in Motherhood program, which gives funds to mothers to complete an artist residency in their own home and community. I'm also really drawn to the Mother House Studios project in the UK, the first artists' studios with integrated childcare.

Initiatives like these create spaces to show each other how it can work, opening the doors to our own processes, inviting women to share in the journey of figuring it out. Visibility, alongside frankness and intimacy, creates a village for both new mothers and women who are deciding whether to have children. These spaces have big potential to show us that it can be done, and create a peer-to-peer approach where an intergenerational support network is possible.

I've learnt from friends like Lisa that in order to reduce the effects of social isolation in motherhood, we must continue to be visible to each other, no matter how imperfect that might look. I try hard now to share how I make it work with the women in my own communities, with my family, clients, and friends and strangers online.

Becoming visible has meant learning to be kinder to myself as I figure it out my own way, knowing that each time I find something that works, I can make the path a little brighter for the next woman, and for the women after her. Our lives can become an offering towards a culture where intimacy and wellbeing take the place of shame, and the simple act of sharing reminds us of the joy.

Rose Ricketson, producer and mother of two

Relationships, intimacy and sexuality

I often forget what James and I did all day before we had children. That life somehow feels further away than my own childhood.

The other day I opened the folder in my Google photos marked '2013', the year before Camille was born. There we were: lying in Central Park with the Sunday papers, on a beach in Montauk, 3 am at a dive bar, riding across the Williamsburg Bridge, drinking good wine out of plastic cups on a friend's rooftop. Ten years and a lifetime ago.

Today we stumble out of bed around 6 am if we're lucky, 5 am if we're not, and fall into the battleground of school lunches, outfit negotiations, beds to be made, hair to be done, shoes to be found, porridge strewn all over the floor, someone crying and a washing machine that won't stop beeping. In one breath I ask James to please cut Freddie's fruit down the middle so he doesn't choke at kinder, check Camille has her piano books, arrange Audrey's extra swimming lesson, remember I'm going out for dinner and to please, please, please listen to that parenting podcast I sent him last week. We'll often argue about something. If we're lucky we'll both have time to shower. On the really good days there'll be a family dance party. And that's all before 8 am. By nightfall, it's rare for us to have had a conversation or sent a text message that didn't begin with, 'How long did Freddie nap?' or 'Any ideas for dinner?' or 'What time will you be home?'

Sustaining a relationship in the midst of this crazy ride takes an immense amount of time, work, gratitude, understanding and respect and sometimes, even with all of that, relationships end. Decades of research backs up what parents know all too well: partnerships suffer when children come along, for obvious reasons – there's far less sleep, changes in sexual desire, huge identity shifts, unequal division of labour in the home leading to resentment and anger, conflicting parenting styles, financial stress, guilt, childhood triggers, burnout, overwhelm and a lot less time to focus on each other.

When I sit with my doula clients postpartum and hold space as they share what is shifting for them in their relationships, three main themes usually come through: a dramatic shift in sexual desire and capacity, a sense of feeling undervalued and unacknowledged in their newfound mother/care role and financial tension, especially when the birthing person takes off more time than their partner, has a period of no income and there are separate bank accounts involved. It's important to talk about these potential conflicts before babies come along – before you're exhausted, angry and upset. But if you didn't, there's no better time than now to start the conversation by asking yourself and your partner:

- How do you want to navigate the complex changes to your sexuality and communicate your needs and feelings to your partner?
- How are they feeling about their own sexuality and how has it changed?
- What boundaries will you put in place together?
- How are you as a family going to challenge our cultural undervaluing of the mother role, and how will you work as a team to differentiate caregiving from domestic duties and, one step further, name and divide them equally?
- How are you feeling about your family's financial situation and your own personal financial situation? Financial abuse is a very real form of family violence. You should have access to money at all times and if you're feeling that the distribution of finances in your family is unfair or even abusive, tell someone and seek support (1800 RESPECT in Australia).

During the first six months of motherhood I developed a resentment towards my partner that I didn't expect to feel. We are very close and open with each other and I didn't think I could ever feel so agitated or angry with him, especially when he wasn't doing anything wrong, but I did. I was frustrated that he could sleep through our daughter's cry, I was annoyed that he could leave the house at a moment's notice, I felt angry that my pelvic floor was weak, my breasts sore and my libido gone while his body stayed the same. That season has passed, gradually my body healed and I found my way back to myself and to him. Becoming parents in lockdown was hard and amazing. For those months, he was my village. We have emerged from early parenthood as a strong team and I am endlessly proud of the way we look after one another.

"

Beth Ryan
Midwife and mother of Poppy

When you invite another buddy into your party, everything changes, your whole world is disrupted. This is very normal. I like to think of it as an opportunity for partnerships to level up in terms of communication, intimacy, authenticity and the deepening of teamwork and collaboration. It's insane to think you can put your partnership on the backburner and expect it to be intact in five years. Your success is determined on helping each other out. I also think it's really important to normalise the disruption and how scary it can be. Then, in the moments when you feel like killing your partner, you're not also wondering, 'What's fundamentally wrong with us?'

"

Kara Hoppe
Psychotherapist, author, teacher and
mother of Jude and Dion

James and I are still very much in love but we have fought hard for that love. We've had to reconcile our vastly different parenting styles – I worry obsessively about everything that could ever possibly go wrong and he's often up a ladder or a tree or doing something else I think is far too dangerous when he's the only one home with our children – and try to find middle ground. My mind is swamped with guilt he'll never understand and an invisible load he'll never see and at the same time I appreciate there is also immense pressure on him. When I talk about something that's upsetting me or that I need more support with, he usually takes it as a criticism that he isn't doing enough rather than working with me to change the things that need to be changed and together look for solutions – I think this is our greatest challenge and one I am not sure how to resolve. I see and appreciate everything he does – he is an incredible father and an incredible partner. But some days I need more – some days I feel as if I am literally carrying a load so great it might crush me and I have no choice but to ask for more from him even though I see he is also at capacity. I don't have any answers, it's an ongoing struggle.

Sex and intimacy are different too. We're bad at organising date nights and I find him sexiest when he's slow-cooking dinner at 7 am. Intimacy has become a knowing smile across our ransacked living room, or when he reaches his hand across to hold mine at night while we're sitting on opposite ends of the couch watching *The Office* or something else that requires little energy to enjoy. After each of our babies I have needed time and space to come back to myself – to reconcile the mother/lover tug of war and find a way to move my mind and body from one to the other and back again – and each time he's waited for me on the other side. I still feel very much in the depths of postpartum and some days struggle with being touched out and needed so much in a physical sense. Other days, I crave closeness and connection. Like so many couples with young children, we do our best to make space for each other and we know the importance of modelling a sense of safety, respect and love within a relationship for our children. The exhaustion is real, and there is always at least one child between us, but through it all we have worked hard to always find our way back to each other.

Everything in our relationship has changed because we have changed – it's no longer just the two of us reading the papers in Central Park on a Sunday. Now it's movie nights and swimming lessons and birthday parties and pancakes and work and anxiety and school runs and holding three little people as they grow in this world. The relationship we have now is infinitely more challenging but it's also stronger and more honest. James held me as I birthed all three of our babies and on the difficult days I go back to those moments and remember how I felt: safe, supported, loved and honoured. I fall more in love with him every time he calls Freddie 'my darling boy' or waits patiently for Camille to make her next chess move or spends an afternoon in the garden planting sunflowers with Audrey. Most people would describe him as practical but I see him as a dreamer. We live in an old cramped two-bedroom house and, although I recognise our immense privilege, some days that feels hard. We don't have a secret to what has kept us together and we're not perfect. But as challenging as it is, I keep fighting for us because it feels right and I feel safe and I feel loved. And because I love him. I'm proud of us for getting this far.

I think it's important to let mums know that if they are not up for sex, that's okay. It can be so hard to switch from the mother archetype to the lover archetype, especially after the first baby because we literally move into the mother archetype overnight and that is a huge identity shift. It's also completely normal to desire intimacy and sex in the early days postpartum and what can often happen and is rarely spoken about is that women have the libido but men don't. I think however it plays out for you, try to keep intimacy at the top of your list of priorities. It's the little things: saying hello and goodbye, kissing, having a cuddle before you go to sleep. It adds up.

"

Juliet Allen
Sexologist and mother of Milli and Sol

I think we assume that sex and intimacy will get easier as our children get older, that when we don't have a little person on us at all times or co-sleeping next to us then we'll have more space and time and naturally happen upon sex again. Actually, how much you are needed doesn't really change. What changes as they grow up is that now you have people who are more aware and who know exactly where you are and what's going on and who stay up later than you. It actually gets more complicated and you need to decide what to do with that. Motherhood doesn't have to be in the way of incredible intimacy and sexuality and connection with the person that you chose to spend your life with. That you chose to create life with. You chose them first, remember? And yet often what happens in parenthood is we become so child-centric that our needs as women are at the very bottom. The greatest gift that any of us can give our children is a blueprint of love that chooses the lovers – the woman, the man, whoever is in that relationship – as central to the functioning of a healthy developed human who is full of respect and integrity.

The worst thing we can do is shelve this huge aspect of ourselves. I have spoken to women who not only don't eat or eat the scraps off their toddler's plates but who will literally eat the food that's fallen on the floor. We do that with our sex and our intimacy and with our partner too. What we say and do versus what we are feeling and processing and not expressing will print in our children's bodies. What will show up in their relationships when they leave our care is what they have experienced and what they know love to be.

99

Julie Tenner
Intimacy and relationship coach, doula and
mother of Heath, Jade, Lola and Gwen

Our bodies, self-care and rest

When I first became pregnant I knew my body would go through a radical transformation and then I would birth and take some time to recover. I was prepared for that. It's everything that came after – the extreme sport that is mothering and the ongoing physical changes postpartum – that I was a lot less prepared for and, honestly, often shocked by.

I have spent eight years feeding, rocking, bouncing, soothing and carrying my children. Eight years of the hardest physical labour of my life. Eight years of being touched. Eight years of being needed. Eight years of pushing a baby in the stroller or carrying a child in my arms or both. Eight years of interrupted sleep. Eight years of always being there and always being on.

My back aches. I work hard to keep my pelvic floor strong. I have tiny wisps of new baby-fluff hair around my temples following three episodes of postpartum hair loss. My cycle is shorter and my periods are heavier. My breasts are forever changed. My clothes don't fit the way they once did so I'm currently searching for my new style. My mind is often foggy. But ultimately, I am proud of my body. I'll never forget what it has accomplished – the softness of pregnancy, the rawness of birth, the tenderness of postpartum, the intensity of mothering. Every line, stretch and ripple reminds me of the life I have lived and the three babies I have grown, birthed, fed and loved. And in a world that doesn't honour the postpartum body – a world that demands we bounce back and hide the evidence of what we have been through and are going through – it feels like a radical act to embrace mine.

Through it all, I have come to learn that the greatest acts of self-care a mother can do, for herself and for her children, are to honour her body, prioritise her needs and to find time to rest. The need for rest is real. Rest is valuable and important and necessary. We must reject the cultural story that our needs don't matter and that rest can only happen when all the jobs are done (and we all know the jobs are never done). We must show our children that we matter. We must put our needs first as much as humanly possible while also tending to the very real needs of our children. I know it's not always easy to pull this off. I know that some days it feels like an act of self-care just to go to the toilet as soon as you need to. But remember, it's okay to put yourself first. It's okay to need space. Caring for yourself is not going to hurt anyone – in fact, taking care of your emotional and physical needs is actually the best thing you can do for your family. Take care of yourself and your children will thrive off your energy. Honouring your needs will imprint deeply on them and through you they will learn to honour and care for themselves. This matters. You matter. This makes a difference.

Research has shown that girls, more than boys, notice that their emotions, words and feelings have an effect on people. And that we begin, at a young age, to not say what we are feeling because we don't want to upset others. The process is called self-silencing and the link between self-silencing and depression is significant. One of the saddest things I find is that even when we find ourselves in a place where we feel safe enough to share how we are feeling about motherhood, we share and it just isn't met in the way we need. We say, 'I'm finding this really hard', and we are told, 'Oh, don't worry, it will pass so quickly'. That response silences her. We need to be able to say, 'I hate this and I love this', and be met where we are at.

"

Amy Taylor-Kabbaz
Author, journalist, matrescence activist
and mother of Scarlett, Greta and Cassius

Anxiety and depression

When I became a mother I became vulnerable in a way I had never known before. I had everything to lose now that I had a child and the feeling intensified with each baby.

I was and still am terrified of something happening to them and terrified of leaving them if something were to happen to me. I think about it all the time. What would happen if I died? Who would know them and love them the way I do? I am often overcome by the darkest of thoughts. James and I have an unspoken rule that he must text me as soon as he arrives anywhere with our children. The minute he leaves with them, whether it's for a long drive or just to the park, I start catastrophising horrible scenarios in my mind. I spiral with intrusive thoughts. My anxiety is heightened. There is a moment of relief when the text comes but then I begin to worry about all the other things that could happen when they are away from me. When they are at school and kindergarten and I hear an ambulance scream past I fear the worst. I think about families who have experienced tragedies years after reading about them in the newspaper. Postpartum anxiety and depression have ebbed and flowed throughout my motherhood journey. I have found they are at their worst when I am particularly exhausted and also when I am in the process of and just after weaning. It took me a long time to link weaning to the darkness I was experiencing but it is indeed a common experience. So is prenatal depression, which is not spoken about nearly as much as postpartum depression and so often comes as a shock when it does happen.

I never wanted anxiety or depression to be a part of my story so it took me a long time to admit that I needed help. I now have good support and James is attuned to me. I have good days and bad days. At the moment they are mostly good days. I am slowly weaning Freddie and while I do feel the familiar clouds coming back, I am more able to sit in that space with the knowledge that I will hopefully come out the other side as my hormones balance. For me, the hard part is trying to work out what is my anxiety and what are normal motherhood fears. Does every mother worry and spiral with the blackest of thoughts? Are they a consequence of loving our babies with everything we have and everything we are? I'm not sure, but I am working with a psychologist to help answer this question. If you also feel you can't tell the difference, it might be worth talking to your doctor and getting a referral to see a specialist.

Worldwide, an estimated one in ten women suffer from postpartum depression and many of those suffer from anxiety as well. Postpartum psychosis affects one to two women in every thousand. Suicide is one of the leading causes of maternal death worldwide. Mothers are suffering, for all the reasons I have covered in this book and more. There is simply not enough support. We need to build communities around our mothers. We need to be fed, held and heard. We need our institutions and governments to recognise the sanctity of family life and ensure paid leave for both parents is the bare minimum of what they offer. We need to take up space with our stories and share what's going on for us so that we all feel less alone.

I hope that in a small way the stories I have shared in this book and the stories from other mothers have supported you. More than anything, know that you are not alone in what you are feeling. Even the very blackest of thoughts have been thought by another mother. Please get help if you think you need it (in Australia call PANDA on 1300 726 306), it is available to you and there is absolutely no shame in doing so. In fact, it might be the most important thing you do for yourself and for your children.

COURTNEY'S STORY

I was twenty-three when I became pregnant with my first baby. I was young, carefree and deeply in love with my partner, Michael. I felt incredibly lucky to have found someone I wanted to spend the rest of my life with, to be starting a family and becoming a mother – a role that felt so natural to me having grown up with lots of younger siblings. I could not have been happier or more excited for what was to come.

And then, within weeks of becoming pregnant, I started having thoughts and feelings I had never experienced before. A wave of anxiety took hold of me, tightening its grip over my mind. For the first time in my life I could not control the thoughts that entered my mind, nor could I shake the dark thoughts out. I started fixating on death. I obsessed about my grandparents and how they were getting older; how their lives were nearing the end. I couldn't pass elderly people without feeling a tightening in my heart and tears welling up in my eyes. I thought about my own life and the new life I was creating. I thought about the thousands of generations of humans who came before us and all the generations yet to come – the world so enormous and one life so insignificant. I became so fixated on these thoughts that I wasn't able to find joy in the life I was living. To add to this, I began worrying about my worrying. I started feeling incredibly guilty, worried that my thoughts would have a negative impact on my baby's health and development. I also worried I was ruining the joy of pregnancy for both Michael and myself.

I soon started worrying about Michael's health and safety. I cried when he left for work every day with terrible, tragic scenarios playing out in my head. I tried to speak to Michael about it but I couldn't even begin to explain it, and he just couldn't understand. I wished I could play my thoughts on a projector for him so that he could reassure me and tell me how silly they were. I tried my hardest to pull myself together, to think happy thoughts; to think of anything else.

A friend once told me that thinking about death was like trying to stare at the sun; both are extremely difficult for humans to do. But here I was obsessing about death. Staring straight at it, unable to turn away.

Our baby, Easton, was born on an especially warm and sunny June day, right on time. After a long labour he arrived quickly and beautifully, and his perfect tiny body was placed on my chest. Instantly, almost unbelievably, as if I had simultaneously pushed out all negative thoughts with my baby, my mind returned to normal.

The Motherhood Space

Thoughts, both happy and sad, would come and go in the same, healthy way they did before I became pregnant. I felt joy like I've never felt in my life and, of course, immense relief to have control over my mind again. It is a testament to the power of hormones that a switch inside your mind can be triggered during pregnancy and immediately switched off at pregnancy's end.

When I was pregnant with Easton I did not know that depression or anxiety could take place during pregnancy. I had heard about postpartum depression, but nobody had ever spoken about depression during pregnancy. I remember googling about pregnancy depression, hoping to find that it was normal. It was 2004, however, and unlike today, I found few results to help me.

While we've come a long way since then in acknowledging and addressing it, I think there is still a taboo surrounding anxiety in pregnancy. It is meant to be such a happy and hopeful time in life, those suffering it can have a hard time admitting so. As with all aspects of life, it's so nice to share these feelings with others; to know you're not alone. Over the years, I've found that the more I share my experiences, the more common I find them to be. Other people have told me they too suffered with anxiety in pregnancy, or their sister did, or their friend did. A simple Google search today about pregnancy or antenatal depression will thankfully yield results on the topic, which at the very least leads me to know it is normal. I read somewhere that it could even be as many as one in every ten pregnant women who suffer from pregnancy anxiety. I think the best thing we can do if we suffer in any way throughout pregnancy or postpartum is to share, ask questions and to know you're not alone.

Courtney Adamo, blogger, author and mother of Easton, Quin, Ivy, Marlow and Wilkie

If I could go back to my younger self, I'd say: let it go. We can be so hard on ourselves and I think that is to the detriment of both us and our children. Every mother has regrets. Every mother has ambivalence. Every mother gets angry. And that's okay. We need to deconstruct that sanitised perfect mother image that takes up residence in our psyche and be easier on ourselves. We are doing our best.

"

Andrea O'Reilly, PhD
Full professor in the School of Gender, Sexuality and Women's Studies at York University, founder and director of The Motherhood Initiative (1998–2019), founder of the *Journal of the Motherhood Initiative*, editor/author of twenty-five books, publisher of Demeter Press and mother of three

Guilt and being enough

It's Saturday and it's raining.

A cold, middle-of-winter day. We spent the morning at the park. Audrey in her summer dress, as always. Either she doesn't feel the cold or fashion takes priority. Now we are home and Freddie has just woken from his nap. It's my favourite time of day with him. We snuggle on the couch and he breastfeeds and sits still for almost five minutes. The girls are doing a puzzle and everything feels soft and warm. I have to leave soon though. I'm getting closer to this book's deadline and still have a lot to do. I try not to work on the weekend but for these last few months I haven't had a choice. I have to leave. I break up the harmony by putting my coat on and Freddie starts to cry. I have to peel him off me. James says he'll take them to a new playground, the girls seem happy with that but Freddie won't let me go. He does this thing where he taps the spot he wants you to sit, and he's next to the couch tapping furiously. I can't resist.

'Just go,' James says. But it isn't that easy. I eventually calm Freddie by telling him he can wave goodbye to me at the window and maybe spot a truck while he's there. I leave.

My words don't flow that afternoon. I sit there and write and write and write and then delete it all. Nothing makes sense. I miss them. I'm sad about the perfect afternoon I ruined. I love having space to work but when I do I am often met with this crushing guilt. I feel guilty for leaving them. I feel guilty for something most days, whether it's something I did or said or didn't do or a decision I made for them years ago that I'm still thinking about. Did I work too much? Did I hug them enough? Was today too rushed? Did I yell too much? Am I cooking enough healthy food? Did I stop and pay enough attention to that story or that drawing or that rock? Have I given them all enough time? Am I enough?

Guilt is a crushingly common emotion in motherhood. The expectations on us are huge and guilt is an inevitable consequence of that. I've mentioned the good mother narrative many times – the narrative that says we should enjoy motherhood all the time, that we should never feel conflicted or ambivalent or overwhelmed, that we should put everyone's needs before our own, that we shouldn't yell or get upset, that our home should be in perfect order, that we should work as if we're not mothers and we should mother as if we don't work. These socially constructed 'shoulds' are impossible ideals no one can meet, yet they still make up so much of the guilt we carry because we have internalised them since childhood.

When I feel guilty today, I try to interrogate where it's coming from: is it mine and tied to my values or is it a result of this good mother narrative? I don't want to be a martyr for my children. I want them to know I am human. I want them to see me make mistakes and I want them to know that sometimes I struggle and can't always be there and don't always know what to do – because then, hopefully, they will mirror that in themselves and know that it's okay to be flawed, that no one is perfect. All mothers feel guilt but I think it's time we rewrite this good mother narrative with grace and humour and the truth about how hard this all is so that when we do feel that guilt rising up we can own it as a normal human emotion rather than a construct of patriarchal motherhood.

Guilt and motherhood are one and the same. Women are judged in a way that men are not. You can be a bad father and still be a good man. If you're a bad mother, you are a bad woman. The expectations on us are so much higher.

"

Andrea O'Reilly, PhD
Full professor in the School of Gender, Sexuality and Women's Studies at York University, founder and director of The Motherhood Initiative (1998-2019), founder of the *Journal of the Motherhood Initiative*, editor/author of twenty-five books, publisher of Demeter Press and mother of three

The perfect mother myth sets up a facade of who we need to be as mothers: we need to work and contribute to our family and show our children what it looks like to be a working mother but never put work first. We should always be happy, never lose our patience, never experience ambivalence or conflicting feelings. We should feel we are made for this, that we have instincts and know how to follow them. We should please everyone all the time and be a great wife and contributor to our community. We know from research that internalising the perfect mother myth impacts a mother's mental and physical health and wellbeing. An alternative I like to talk about is 'good enough' mothering – originally coined by paediatrician and psychoanalyst Donald Winnicott – which is just as important for our children's development as it is for our identity and development as mothers. Our job is to raise our children to be human beings and how we do that is by being human ourselves.

"

Dr Sophie Brock
Motherhood studies sociologist and mother of one

MALWINA'S STORY

'Does he have a high-sugar diet?' The dentist asks the trick question after looking up from my seven-year-old's mouth. Answer yes and I've failed because I am a bad mother, giving my child candy. Answer no and also fail, because childhood is precisely the time to enjoy a high-sugar diet. Life is short, they grow up so fast, the world is ending anyway – a choose-your-own dental adventure! 'If we were to compare, I would say my other child is more likely to qualify as a high-sugar diet candidate,' I answer, sacrificing my then-four-year-old, who was still young enough to not care about the dentist's judgement, so I wouldn't be alone under the weight of condemnation.

Years flash before my eyes and I am back to my own childhood in Canada, in the days when a dentist would visit our school every few weeks. I dreaded those visits as, one by one, we got called in. She made children cry, accusing us of terrible dental atrocities, while the hygienist, the 'nice one', held our hands. I was seven when I associated cavities with shame and was the only girl in Grade 1 who had a tooth extracted at school. I didn't even get to keep it like the other kid, a boy, who came back to class proudly toting his pulled tooth in a plastic pill vial. My tooth was too rotten to save, the dentist said. My mum, as most mums, blamed herself for letting me drink Coca-Cola whenever I wanted. It was an immigrant thing, she tells me to this day. 'We never had sweet things when I was a child in Poland, so I wanted you to have everything you wanted.'

One of my least favourite parental duties is helping my children brush their teeth. Apart from the obvious logistical complications – asking children to open mouths wide, getting to the back without making anyone gag, remembering to brush at all – I don't want to be dentist-shamed if my children get cavities. And then there is the tooth fairy, a magic I love, a responsibility I loathe. There are few things that make me as anxious as trying to slip my hand under my child's pillow while he sleeps to make the money-for-tooth exchange.

Two days after his sixth birthday, my son lost his first tooth. By lost, I mean it fell out and he swallowed it. For a week after, my partner and I looked for the tooth in his poo every night, using small sticks to sift through the shit. My son loves popcorn, especially the crunchy un-popped kernels. There was a lot of confusion that week regarding what was a baby tooth and what was in fact a kernel. In the end, we gave up – there were a lot of kernels and no teeth.

The Motherhood Space

There are two dental fricatives in the English language: ð (eth), like in 'the', 'this' and 'teething'; and θ (theta), like in 'think' and, yes, 'teeth'. The two sounds are made by placing the tip of the tongue between the teeth. The former is voiced, the latter, voiceless. Like most young kids, my daughter struggles with the th sound. It often makes her cry when we are working through a learn-to-read book and I ask her to practise th or try to read 'this' or 'that'. Th-fronting is the pronunciation of th as f or v, a common feature of various English dialects like Cockney, Essex and Estuary English. It is not a feature of Received Pronunciation, also known as the Queen's English, a dialect associated with upper- and upper-middle classes. As a Canadian in London, it did not take long to witness the prevalence of the perceived link between accent or dialect, and social class, a British obsession, as well as the pervasiveness of accentism, discrimination based on someone's accent or language use. Last year, while waiting for my daughter at swimming, a father was leaving with his young son, three, maybe four years old. 'It is not "fing", it's "thing"!' the father said. 'Look at where my tongue touches my teeth.' I wanted to scream at the father that th-fronting was common and age-appropriate for children his son's age, and to give the kid a break. Instead, I gritted my teeth and turned away.

'Your teeth are chipping because you grind at night,' says my dentist. 'You really need to wear a dental guard while you sleep.' I got a dental guard, its high cost partially covered by the UK's National Health Service (NHS), the publicly funded healthcare system. Now, when I wake up with customary 3 am anxiety, I run my tongue against the smooth surface of the night-guard, willing the action to help me fall back asleep.

Earlier this year, my dentist gave up his NHS contract, meaning his dental practice is now fully private and a child's fifteen-minute dental check is £50 out-of-pocket. At 3.15 am, I begin to worry I am grinding so much that holes will soon appear in the dental guard. How much will a new one cost now?

And I can't forget to find a new dentist for my children tomorrow.

Malwina Gudowska, linguist and mother of two

Mothering outside the nuclear narrative

We have been conditioned as a society to view the heteronormative nuclear family narrative to be the norm and desirable.

If we interrogate this, the message being sent to us for generations is that there is a right way to do this parenting thing and anything outside of that is somehow less – what a huge and unwelcome burden that message puts on women whose paths are different from the one set by our society. To the solo mothers, queer mothers, stepmothers, co-parenting mothers, mothers whose partners have died, adoptive mothers and any other mother who might feel unseen and under-represented on this journey: I hope as we slowly emerge out of the shadow of the patriarchy you feel the burden and stigma lift as well. I am in awe of you and all you do.

Thank you Ellie, Hazel and Amy for sharing your stories.

ELLIE'S STORY

I can already see her in the future telling her friends about her big modern family. She'll be smiling while she explains that although her parents haven't been together for years, they are great friends.

As she scans through her childhood memories, we'll both be around, making jokes, teasing, watching her tricks. And as she continues to get older, it'll be all of us, cheering from the sidelines of her sports, or interest that she chooses.

There will be grandparents and aunties, uncles, some by blood and some just by love and step-parents and siblings. And us.

She'll have a beautiful stepmother who'll braid her hair for her (probably better than I can, I'm working on it), snuggle her up when she is feeling unwell and read her stories at night before sleep. A stepmother who will love her and treat her as her own, and I'd expect nothing less.

She'll have a stepdad to fix her broken toys and wrap around her finger to the point of no return.

She'll have more grandparents, cousins and siblings than she could have ever imagined. There will be so much love, and she'll be right smack in the middle of it.

And one day, we'll all be hanging out together, and she'll look around and she'll know that all these people have come together for her, that our love conquers all. And we'll have navigated, journeyed, and ridden the ups and downs of this not-so-trodden path together to allow this.

And my most favourite vision, the one I think about almost daily, is the one where she turns around from whatever she is doing and sees us all sitting around together chatting and laughing and she knows that the big, beautiful family we have created is all because of her.

Ellie Lemons, mother of Rocky

HAZEL'S STORY

My experience of motherhood was diving into the deep end and realising I was not a very good swimmer. When I met my wonderful husband, he was a father of three with full custody. We got married eight months after we met, had our first baby within the first year and our second a year after that. Within two years, I was a mum of five. My journey has been an ongoing battle – a journey of being stubborn as hell and standing up for them. We have neurodiversities throughout our family and our children are challenging and amazing. When our youngest got her first suspension from school, rather than being distraught, we said, 'Congratulations! You are the last one in the family to get this! Well done!'

They have struggled because of their neurodiversity and I have had to fight just to keep them in school and to get them the support they need. When we got our first autism diagnosis, my son was five and we were told by his private school, 'We'll keep all your normal children here but you need to take out your abnormal child.' So I went around to every single classroom and got all my kids out and we left that day. When you believe in your children and are their advocate, you see the wins. My daughter is now in Year 8 and just in the last month has had one hundred wins. Most parents would see these wins as normal: getting herself to school, wanting to be at school, making good friends and planning social activities. She's going shopping with friends this weekend and that is huge for her, but she's not going to get any rewards or school recognition for those achievements. School has never focused on her strengths, only ever on her issues. So you have to be the mama bear – fight for them and celebrate them.

Dr Hazel Keedle, midwife, author, researcher and mother of five

AMY'S STORY

As the separation unfolded in front of my eyes I found myself asking:

Will I be good enough?

Will I be able to hold them through this?

Will I be able to stay present to them, and to the reality of this moment, and also find space to soothe and attend to what this is stirring up from my own childhood?

So many questions, but at the core, these two:

Will they break?

Will I break?

I look back to her – to the version of me from a few years ago – with such a sense of compassion and reverence. I realise now that I was doing an amazing job navigating incredibly tough terrain.

As for those two questions that rolled round my mind during that time ...

They did break, in a way.

So did I.

And: that doesn't have to be a bad thing.

What I've been most surprised by in my transition to single mothering/co-parenting is how different my lived experience of single mothering is from what our cultural and societal narrative tells us.

In our current culture and society, single mothering is an unquestionably unfavourable situation for mothers to be in.

Mothers within nuclear families quietly (or even subconsciously) say, 'I'm glad that's not me', and 'I don't know how she does it', about their single mothering counterparts. And I know they do, because I did too. When you're in a nuclear family structure, it's difficult to imagine there is any other way.

When we talk of single mothering in our cultural narrative, we talk about the difficulty of navigating night-times or achieving anything with just one set of arms. We talk of the stretch that comes when illness strikes, the emotional load, the exhaustion and the loneliness.

But if we're really being honest, even within the perceived safety of the nuclear family structure, many mothers are navigating night-times solo. They're already the ones juggling sickness within the family. They're already stretched, and exhausted and carrying a significant emotional and mental load. Many mothers are already lonely.

What I realised as my own path unfolded is that in reality, it's not so black and white. Most of the things I had feared about single mothering were already a part of my existence within the nuclear family.

We talk about the very real financial difficulties that single mothers face. This cannot be understated. Mothers have often been out of the workforce for their mothering work, and, in cases of separation, holding and tending to the emotional and mental load of separation. Alongside all this big work is a feeling of pressing financial pressure. A pressure to get back on their feet and into the workplace in order to pay the rent. It's rough and I will not downplay the reality of the financial disadvantage that stepping away from the dual income household can bring.

But single mothering and single motherhood bring enrichment and beauty too. And this is the part we never talk about.

For me, like so many others, single mothering and co-parenting has created freedom and freshness and expansion in myself and within our family structure.

The honest truth is that I can love my kids more freely now.

I feel a sense of independence and self-guidance in the course of our days and months. I have found a deeper sense of community now than I ever would have if I remained in the nuclear family structure. My kids and I go around to the friends up the road for dinner. Other single mums and I go for walks when we're kid-free. It feels honest and whole and real and often incredible.

I am less lonely now than when I was inside the structure of the nuclear family.

The growth hasn't come without real work. It's taken time and reflective practice and therapy. Working with a psychologist has allowed me to get to know myself in a way I might never have if I had stayed insulated and buffeted by the nuclear family dynamic.

If I'm honest, despite the hard and the heartbreak, I'd choose this life over again.

That doesn't mean I don't think about the reality of the financial position I find myself in. But this life still ends up coming up a win.

If you ever find yourself in the position of becoming a single mother, I want to say: do what you need to do in order to steady yourself. Steady your nervous system, and the steadiness of your kiddos will follow.

Looking after yourself is an integral part of looking after your little ones. You will not be able to guide them through this by sacrificing your health and wellbeing. Start with simple things, like making sure you're drinking enough water. Or going for a walk around the block every day. Do what you can to take care of yourself.

If you find your way to single mothering, please remember: you are doing the best you can with what you have. And that is such a gift. Make room for the hard days. The unproductive days. The days where it feels like you've taken twenty steps backwards. Make room for the whole spectrum of days.

In time you'll stand back and survey the whole landscape of your experience. And you will marvel at how you set about forging new ground.

Let it all fall apart. Let the cultural story of The Doomed Single Mother fall away. And, in your own time, you will create something that's entirely new. Something entirely beautiful.

Amy O'Brien, Chinese herbalist, acupuncturist, birth support person, motherhood studies practitioner and mother of Jimmy and Wallis

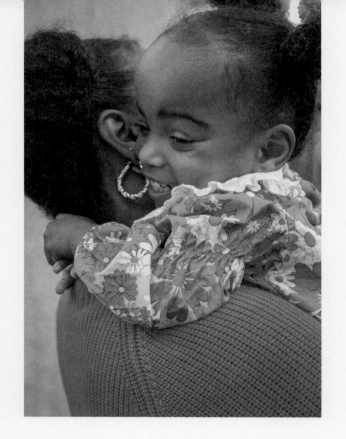

There is nothing like parenthood to bring up your own childhood. You could have done a good solid ten years in psychotherapy and still become a mother or a father and find yourself in a washing machine of triggers for different reasons – whether it's you interacting with your child or watching your partner interact with your child. It's so important not to minimise the discomfort but to normalise it – it's okay!

"

Kara Hoppe
Psychotherapist, author, teacher and
mother of Jude and Dion

Imprints and healing our wounds

Parenthood offers a unique opportunity to re-parent ourselves alongside our children and to break cycles of generational patterns that have not served you.

It's natural and inevitable that your own childhood experiences – good and bad – will resurface when you become a parent. You will be triggered time and time again, there is no way to avoid this. What you do with that, though, will depend on how much awareness and support you have to acknowledge your triggers and recognise that they don't have to be a part of your own parenting story. We didn't bring our children into this world to project our past hurt onto them so that they carry these wounds and cycles into the next generation. We have an opportunity to step back and let them be, to watch them grow and learn and make their own mistakes while we grow and relearn and heal beside them. The things you do every day in your home, welcoming your children as they are and making space for their big feelings and reminding them they are safe and that their whole selves are welcome – that they don't have to be a good boy or a good girl to be loved – will slowly but surely build the foundations for healthy emotionally intelligent children while simultaneously breaking the cycles of generations past. This work won't be easy and it won't be quick, but it is important and necessary and it is work we all have a responsibility to do.

Here's the reality. Your kids are going to have stories and will have to navigate adversity and tricky stuff no matter what you do because they are human, and they actually need to develop these life skills. So take the pressure off having to be perfect. There is no perfect. The more you do the work on yourself the easier ride your children are going to have because you are not going to project all your shit onto them. The biggest gift you can give your children is to do your own work. Look at the stories you were raised with, look at the stories you are continuing now and look at where you are not feeling your feelings, because they are constantly watching you and their imprint of what it is to be a human in the world is forming right now and if we are sitting in these cycles of blame or guilt or shame or not good enough, that is the imprint we pass on to them no matter what.

"

Lael Stone
Speaker, author, educator, creator and
mother of Ky, Indi and Tali

AMALIE'S STORY

Nothing has taught me more in life than becoming a mother. In 2017, when pregnant with our first girl, the sense of motherhood started for me. We lost her after eighteen weeks in my womb.

This tremendous and traumatic experience left me in awe of nature's brutal but calm order of life and the lessons it taught me knitted my husband and me closer together.

I felt the presence of nature speaking to me during this process. I felt like a sheep that had lost its lamb, mourning and searching for the purpose of being. I felt the great power of nature, the unstoppable force – no matter how much I wanted it to stop. Never have I lived more in the present. Never have I loved my husband deeper.

One year later we became parents to our daughter, Bobbie. With deep wisdom, a calm spirit and eyes like the sea, she came and turned my world around.

I haven't looked into myself that deeply before. Everything I knew now had new meaning, and many things I thought I loved faded away. I saw myself clearer than ever in the light of her. More than ever, I wanted to heal my own trauma and the thought of passing it onto her was the scariest thing I ever experienced.

Three years later, in the winter of 2022, I became pregnant with our third baby girl. I felt her before she was even in my belly. She has been in my head for a while, maybe a year, maybe forever, but I wasn't ready before now. I knew that I would learn something new in this pregnancy as well, and I was curious to find out what – I knew that it would change me, but how?

Today I find myself face to face with my own inner child. For the very first time in my twenty-nine years, I feel and recognise her. I feel her searching for trust and security more than ever before. I feel able to make decisions that would have calmed her back then, because today I am responsible and I am in charge.

I don't miss my old self. What does that even mean? Motherhood has taught me to be responsible for my own feelings and it has taught me that nature has an unstoppable rhythm. I am the same as before but motherhood has shaped me into my authentic self. I can now see my true identity, my fears and my faults. This makes me more grounded and rooted than ever before. I am not complete, nor am I perfect.

I am in awe of nature, motherhood and beyond. Finally, I have become the person I am – for my daughters.

Amalie Reedtz-Thott, mother nature nurse and mother of two

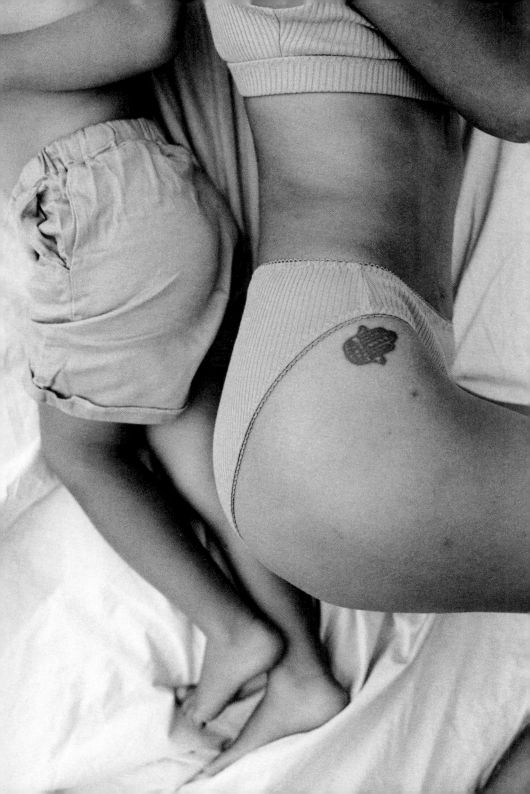

To mother is to nurture, to nourish, and to care for with dedication and commitment. It is also a journey of personal growth, enabling many opportunities for self-awareness and red thread or mother-line healing.

"

Jane Hardwicke Collings
Women's mysteries teacher, shamanic craftswoman, midwife, writer, teacher, mother and grandmother

Mothering
without mothers

The need to be mothered never leaves us, even
and perhaps especially as we age and birth our
own babies and grow into the identity ourselves.

We look to those who raised us and we see them in a whole new light,
with a fresh perspective and a new understanding of who they are and what
they have experienced. When that love and guidance is taken away, through
death or circumstance, the pain, I can only imagine, is deep and immense.
A unique and complex grief.

To Chloe and Dusk, thank you for sharing these beautiful and tender stories
of your mothers and how they have shaped your own motherhood journeys.

CHLOE'S STORY

My dreams of how motherhood might be for me were violently disrupted when my mum passed away suddenly. I was fourteen weeks pregnant with my first child.

My mum was a very hands-on, loving mother. A paediatric nurse, she was so confident and natural with kids and was ecstatic about the news of my pregnancy – my daughter was to be her first grandchild.

From the moment I learnt she had died, I was instantly protective of my baby, which was the pattern for the rest of my pregnancy and postpartum. I carried dual feelings of intense loss and a striving to hold grief at bay lest it affect my little girl, alongside the happy hormones of pregnancy. It was a wild ride. It took a lot of strong self-talk, therapy and leaning on my village to constantly remind me that my baby and I would be okay.

A week before my daughter was due, my mum's mother, my nana, also passed away. My little girl arrived into the world at the exact moment my nana's funeral service ended, in a truly spine-tingling gift of circumstance. As I lay on the bed being prepped for my caesarean, I had the intense feeling that my mum, grandparents and my dad (who had died ten years ago) were holding hands around me. It's an image I return to in my head over and over for comfort, as it was so powerful and vivid.

Mothering without my mother has been a mix of intense emotions. Some days I look at my daughter and can feel my mum and my nana within her, and I feel so grateful to have her here to anchor me and keep me filled with love and endorphins during what could be an overwhelmingly sad time. Other days I feel so sad that my mum can't share in the joy of her. Mum would have loved her so much. And I constantly wonder how she felt when I was little – the choices she made, the challenges she faced, how she felt being a new mum. I'll never know, but I hope I'll keep reflecting.

I named my daughter Ellie Lea, after my mum, Lea.

Surrounding myself with a supportive village felt even more important without my mum. I engaged a postpartum doula and rallied my friends as much as possible. My husband was and is an incredible support.

The day my mum died, my nana told me that my mum's cells and my nana's cells existed within my baby and that I must always remember that. In that way, Mum and Nana live on in Ellie, and hopefully, I can continue their legacy of being strong, generously loving, warm women.

Chloe Elliot, marriage celebrant and mother of Ellie Lea

DUSK'S STORY

The year I became a mother was the year I said goodbye to my own – my matrescence woven together with birth and death, grief and joy.

Diagnosed with stage 4 cancer, my mum needed a hysterectomy and surgery to remove the spreading tumours. As I sat by her hospital bed I shyly passed her a card. She opened it and read, 'Dear Mum, I honour your womb for carrying me and thank it for all it has held. On this day, as we farewell your womb, mine is filled with life.'

Mum took a moment, sighing as I acknowledged the removal of my first home. Then she paused, a lifetime of longing held within that space. She looked up at me with a smile, 'You're pregnant!?'

I nodded, 'Six weeks.' We cried, squealed with joy and held each other. Three generations embracing in life and loss. Then they wheeled her away.

My next time in hospital was for the birth of my daughter, Skyelar. Beforehand at home, I laboured my daughter into the world over five days of regular contractions. By the third day, they were five minutes apart on the cusp of active labour. A midwife friend came over to support me. Around 1 am, after hours of rhythmic contractions refusing to close in, she tended to my spirit.

'Dusk,' she gently said. 'What are you afraid of?'

In my heart I knew the answer was death. On the precipice of bringing life into the world, I couldn't bear the farewell that awaited me. In the depths of my soul, I was being called to begin the farewell to my mother. I wept in my friend's arms and my fear was met with inner strength. She held me as I transitioned into labour and stepped into the liminal space between life and death to bring my daughter here.

Following the incredible birth of my daughter, we faced a challenging NICU stay. For a dark night we didn't know how our story would end. A week later, we came through the other side and brought a now-healthy baby home. Walking through the door, the last two weeks of labour and NICU heavily weighing on us, our phone rang. It was the news that Mum was not going to make it to the end of the year. I looked down at the baby in my arms, unable to comprehend her beginning at my mother's end.

Six months later, we began my mother's labour towards death. Our relationship had always been complex, with times of closeness and times of separation. I came

The Motherhood Space

to her deathbed with the question: Does Mum love me and does she know that I love her? Mother and daughter, a world held between us.

We held a living funeral for Mum and as we sat together afterwards, I breastfed Skyelar. Her little chubby hand rested on my collarbone, then stroked my chest. My mum gazed at us and softly said, 'You used to do that with me when you were a baby.' For the first time in such a long time, I remembered that I was my mother's daughter. Just as I had grown, birthed and loved Skyelar, my mother had grown, birthed and loved me.

Over the following days and weeks, I visited Mum each day and we simply adored Skyelar together. As I was looking at Skyelar one day, lost in motherhood, my mum whispered, 'It's a love like no other.' Those questions I came with found their home in these quiet moments.

My siblings and I began tending to Mum as she had tended to us so lovingly throughout our childhood. Now I held Mum's hand in my own, singing songs to her that she had sung over me when I was young. The morning of her death, our family huddled around her bed, my daughter, brother, nieces and nephews, partner and sister-in-law. We honoured the body that had carried us. We acknowledged Mum's life and the legacy found in the family surrounding her. Each person's eyes reflected back the life Mum lived of strength, love and joy.

Life after Mum's passing held an emptiness like I had never known. Every day my heart broke with the pain of losing my mother, then was knit back together with the joy of Skyelar. I was a new mother and I was now motherless. My matrescence was entangled with grief, anger and fear. I longed for a reality with my mother that would never be and may never have been. I grieved for what was lost in our relationship over the years. I wished to know her mother to mother. The few months we had left me with a lifetime of questions that will never be answered.

Living through the grief was all-consuming. Pain and longing flowed like breastmilk, holding all of Mum's lasts with all of Skyelar's firsts. As Skyelar would do something for the first time, the pain that Mum was not here to see it broke me. Five years since motherhood was given and daughterhood taken away, the edges of my grief have softened. Slowly over time, I began to feel Mum with us and now we share in Skyelar's joy together. I have come to see my mother in the fullness of her own motherhood.

While I longed to separate my matrescence from grief, becoming a mother will always be intertwined with my mother's death. It was the hardest time of my life, tending to my mother's passing, to the new mother within me and to my little baby. Yet I cherish each of those firsts and lasts that I was present to. Within it, I have come to know motherhood as the tension between many things ... life and death, pain and joy, darkness and light, grief and love. A love like no other.

Dusk Liney, *trauma-sensitive maternal care advocate and mother*

I love that my kids are older now. My eldest are twelve and fourteen and I literally love hanging out with them. We have the best conversations around the dinner table. I am so interested in this generation. They are fascinating and empowered and spectacular and they have been through so much already. And I just sit and listen and think, I birthed you! How amazing!

"

Amy Taylor-Kabbaz
Author, journalist, matrescence activist
and mother of Scarlett, Greta and Cassius

Creating space
and staying close

One of the unexpected joys of writing this book was speaking with women whose children were older than mine.

They gave me insights on parenthood and raising teenagers that I hadn't yet considered and that have helped me so much as I wrestle with the passing of time and how fleeting this all is. When I asked them if they missed their children as newborns and babies and toddlers and young children, they said they did but they no longer longed for them in the way I find myself longing for those days. All of them said something similar and amazing: that the best is yet to come. That every day their children become somehow more wonderful. That every year with them has been better than the last. It reminded me of when Camille was a baby and any time anyone asked me what the best age was I'd always say whatever age she was at that time. At six months: This is the best age! At one year old: No, this is! At eighteen months: It cannot get any better than this! And yet, it always did. It gets better every day.

And so even though I feel an ache when memories come up on my phone and I can't believe how little they were just one year ago, I am now also carrying with me the knowing that some of our best days are coming. That one day soon James and I will be sitting on the couch with our teenagers sharing pizza and watching a show we all love and I'll look around and think: no, this is the best age. And that sounds kind of wonderful. I can't wait for that.

Parenting my son and learning to relish and adore the masculine has been my greatest learning and my greatest reward. He has taught me how to love men beyond my own trauma and my own feminist projections. I have learnt how to be with him without needing to make him 'more sensitive', and how to remove judgement on his competitive and masculine ways of belonging to the world. But the journey has been hard. Eight and nine were my hardest years with him and I remember doing a huge amount of research at this time that centred Indigenous and historical communities' wisdom. What I discovered was, across cultures and traditions, this was a time where boys intuitively 'moved' from being mother-centric to father-centric in their attachment and open up to what it is to be 'man'. Traditionally it would have been a time when they took the boys away to learn 'men's business', survival skills and honed their masculine gifts of integrity and provision. A time they learn to embody 'the warrior'. In Steiner philosophy they call it 'The Crossing'. It was so disruptive – a lot of attitude, backlash and anger – and I see it play out a lot, yet there is no conversation around it. He was absolutely sure about who he was and what he needed and he did not see or experience the world as I did. So I had to do some really intense learning really quickly. I wanted to homebirth and unschool and babywear and he was like give me black, give me white, I love the system, and I love competition and it was a clashing of worlds that was such a disruption to me and my body. But we are through it and it has been the best journey. He's sixteen now and I just love him. He's the most awesome human and I love our relationship.

"

Julie Tenner
Intimacy and relationship coach, doula and
mother of Heath, Jade, Lola and Gwen

It's hard for so many of us to parent teenagers because so much of our own teenage journey was painful. Most of us did not have what we needed back then: a mentor or a guide to give us safety and support so we could be who we needed to be. So of course when our beautiful kids start blossoming into their sexuality, everything we are carrying is going to rise up again. I believe connection is always the answer. We need to keep working on the connection and it is the parents' responsibility to do this, not the child's. So how do we meet them where they are? Be interested in their life without being overbearing? How do we stop nagging and controlling when they are just trying to figure out who they are? Our job is not to fix it. Our job is to be there and to listen. And to be the safe place for them to fall when they fall, because they will.

"

Lael Stone
Speaker, author, educator, creator and
mother of Ky, Indi and Tali

Every age it's amazing to see what she's becoming, but then as a mother, I am losing what was at the same time. She is now five foot ten and I am five seven, so she has outgrown me. When we were eye to eye that was a really strange transition for me, to be outgrown was a really strange experience. Just perceptively, to have someone who can't comfortably sit on my lap, who can't share any of my clothes. But it's awesome parenting a teenager. It's kind of like parenting a toddler. Like my friend said the other day, it's mostly just keeping them alive.

"

Kimberly Ann Johnson
Author, somatic experiencing practitioner, sexological bodyworker, birth doula and mother of Cece

Feeling lost and feeling found

When I was growing up my mum lived for the school holidays.

I watched her as she washed and packed away our bags and lunch boxes and uniforms with a lightness to her being and a huge smile on her face. 'I am so happy to have you all home!' she'd say, and we bathed in her delight. Our dad – wonderful, loving and the kindest man I know – wasn't as present during our childhood. He worked overseas in Indonesia and Vietnam and West Africa and other faraway places for five weeks at a time, each time coming home to a house that had found a whole new rhythm while he'd been away. I know now there were days when Mum felt lost and lonely and trapped and alone, because now we talk about them often. But growing up, all I ever felt was her fierce love and warm dressing-gown hugs and her pure joy when she was with us. Before I became a mother, it was what I hoped to also give my children: a feeling of being absolutely adored. A knowing in their soul that they are so very loved.

Now every time Camille or Audrey or Freddie reach out their hand to hold mine I tell them it is the greatest feeling in the world, having their little hands in mine. I remind them every day how adored they are. They see me get angry, they hear me yell, they know I'm not perfect. But I know beyond a doubt that they know how very loved they are.

Motherhood has been the making of me. I have experienced the highest highs and the lowest lows. I have felt disorientated, frustrated, hopeful, light and loved, sometimes all at once. A few weeks ago, Camille asked if she could sleep with me in the single bed I am currently sleeping in, in their room. I said we probably wouldn't sleep all that well, but she said we would because we'd be close and isn't that the thing that makes us both happiest? So she hopped down off her bunk and into my bed. Six weeks later she is still there.

Let's go to bed, darling.

Everything will be better
in the morning.

Everything is always
better in the morning.

"

Heather Nancarrow
My mother

Sometimes Audrey also gets in. I find myself desperate for space but also not ever wanting these days of them wanting to sleep so close to me to end. Camille gives me a different reason every night for wanting to be in bed with me (it's warmer, the pillow is better, the blankets are softer, the mattress is more comfy) but just last night she turned and said, 'Actually, Mummy, those aren't the reasons. I just want to be close to you.' And so I surrender and hold on to her, just as I am holding on to these days before they slip away (and also wondering if we should buy a double bed, because, sleep).

I feel honoured to be loved and cherished so much. Motherhood. A journey and an invitation into the great unknown. What a wild, wonderful ride.

I hope you have found comfort in these pages. I hope they have made you feel less alone and more understood. I hope they have brought some peace to your chaotic days and supported you to fight for more equality in your life. May we continue to fight the patriarchy so that our daughters are free of everything that has held us back.

My love to you, beautiful mother. You are doing an extraordinary job.

A note to my children

My darling Camille.

One day when you are older, I will remind you of how the flowers smelled that spring you were born and how, one year later, you bent to admire every single one of them on our walks around the neighbourhood. I will remind you of that little crinkle on your nose and that it was the first thing I noticed when you were born and how still to this day I am the only one who can see it. I will remind you of how you became obsessed with Jackson Pollock as a two-year-old when we went down a YouTube rabbit hole one ordinary day, and how you'd sit for hours at the art table Daddy built for you, splattering paint all over the windows and walls saying, 'I'm Jackson Pollocking, Mummy!' You spend less and less time at that art table these days, preferring to draw at our dining room table. I guess you've outgrown those tiny chairs we bought for you five years ago. We are planning to renovate our house soon but I'm not sure how I'll ever part with those paint-splatted windows. One day when you are older, I will remind you of the colour and joy you brought to our days and how you always knew just what I needed. I will remind you how you loved to play with your little sister during playtime at school, even when your friends didn't want to join you, and how you made perfume out of flower petals and once told me that I was your favourite person 'in this whole wide life'. One day when you are older, I will remind you of that funny little dance you did night after night to convince me to read just one more page of *Harry Potter* and I will remind you that you, my darling girl, made me a mother and that together we have learnt so much. I love you.

My darling Audrey.

One day when you are older, I will remind you of how you liked to sleep in your favourite dresses with all your jewellery and your headbands, and how sometimes we even found you in your swimming goggles! One day when you are older, I will remind you how beautiful your soul was from the moment you opened your eyes, how caring you are and how much you cried when the sunflowers died. I will remind you of the time we went to the magic show and they asked you to come up on the stage and you jumped up in front of all those people with such confidence and ease, and how they told you that the only way to find magic is to believe in it. And I will remind you how, months later and minutes before falling asleep, you whispered in my ear that you think of the magic show every night before you fall asleep because it makes you so happy. One day when you are older, I will remind you how I would often find you in the bathroom, deep in my make-up drawer, mascara applied perfectly to your thick black lashes that will never actually need it. I will remind you of how you learnt to write your big sister's name before your own and how you have hugged your baby brother a hundred times a day since he was born and how lucky I have felt bearing witness to the bond the three of you share. One day when you are older, I will tell you again how you have the kindest heart of anyone I have ever known and I'll tell you about the mornings Daddy and I used to turn to each other and smile when you woke us up with your singing. One day when you are older, my darling, I will remind you of how you have carried me through so many hard days just by being your beautiful self. I love you.

The Motherhood Space

My darling Freddie.

One day when you are older, I will share with you the story of your birth and how you were born on the eve of your grandmother's birthday, in a dark quiet room, in the middle of a pandemic. I'll tell you about how our world had been turned upside down until you came along and everything felt right again. One day when you are older, I will remind you about the pretend cups of tea you'd bring me in the shower every morning and how you liked to sleep sideways in our bed and how you'd always ask me for 'one more hug' whenever I left the room, even if I was just going to make your breakfast. One day when you are older, I'll tell you that the second word you ever spoke was 'girls!' and I will remind you of how you would toddle after your big sisters all day long saying, 'Good morning, ladies!' and 'What can I get for you, ladies?' and how their giggles echoed through our home. One day when you are older, I will remind you that your voice was the first one I would hear every morning, a hopeful, 'Mummy?', a whispered, 'I love you'. I will tell you of all the nights we lay awake together and how you never seemed to need much sleep and how the birds sounded at 5 am when we were playing trains on the rug and my eyes stung and you'd never looked so beautiful, all shaggy hair and soft pink cheeks and the biggest smile in the world. I'll never let you forget how deeply nurturing and sensitive you are and how privileged I feel to be raising a boy in this world. One day when you are older, I will share with you how surprised I was when Daddy said, 'It's a boy!' and how overwhelmed and out of my depth I felt and how over time you have taught me to soften even deeper into my knowing that I am enough for you. I love you.

My darling children, one day when you are older, I will remind you that the days we spent together were my favourite days and how even though some of them were long and some of them were hard, it was never because of you. You were always wonderful.

Thank you

To Amalie Reedtz-Thott, Amy O'Brien, Amy Taylor-Kabbaz, Andrea O'Reilly, Beth Ryan, Chloe Elliot, Corinne Milgrom-Marabel, Courtney Adamo, Dusk Liney, Edwina Lee, Elaine Tiong, Ellie Lemons, Emily Williamson, Eve Rodsky, Fairleigh McLaren, Grace Hooper, Greer Kirshenbaum, Hazel Keedle, Heba Shaheed, Holly Norman, Jane Hardwicke Collings, Jessica Hart, Jessie Stephens, Julie Tenner, Juliet Allen, Justina Edwards, Justine Hughes, Kara Hoppe, Kate Bloom, Kate Ellis, Katie James, Kayla Robertson, Kimberly Ann Johnson, Kristy-Lea Brown, Lael Stone, Malwina Gudowska, Melanie Dimmitt, Mia Elliott, Monique Zender, Natasha Priolo, Patty Wipfler, Pippa James, Rachel Reed, Rose Ricketson, Rowena Cooke, Tami Lynn Kent, Sarah Sky, Sophie Brock, Yanika Flynn and Yeong Sassall, thank you for your tender, life-changing words. And thank you to all the women whose images appear in this book, your gracious support means the world to me.

To Alice and the Hardie Grant team, thank you for having faith in this important narrative.

To my beloved Nanny, thank you for refusing to milk the cows that day, and for the millions of other gifts you gave me.

To Mum and Dad, thank you for raising us in a home filled with joy and safety and love and family dinners. Thank you for showing us that relationships don't have to be perfect to be strong and for keeping us all so close. And Mum, thank you for showing me the way.

To Ben, Bell and Moni, thank you for being my best friends and the best uncle and aunties ever. And Bell, thank you for editing this book with Edie napping on your lap.

To James, there is no way I could have written this without you. Raising these three magical souls alongside you has been my greatest achievement and watching you with them, my greatest joy. I love you.

And finally, to the loves of my life, Camille, Audrey and Freddie. Thank you for loaning me to this book for a little while. I hope it's been worthwhile, and I hope that if one day you choose parenthood, my words guide you a little on your journey. It is the best adventure, watching you grow. Thank you for slowing me down and for sprinkling little moments of joy throughout all the days of my life. You are all my dreams come true.

Photography credits

Jessica Sidenros
Front cover.

Becca Crawford
Page 2, 6, 20, 42, 56, 68, 73, 80, 98, 107, 114, 140, 142, 155, 157, 160, 169, 176, 192, 196, 208, 217, 218, 221, 225.

Ilsa Wynne-Hoelscher Kidd
Page 8, 11, 14–15, 32, 45, 59, 63, 64–65, 74, 87, 100, 108, 117, 118–119, 124, 128, 133, 150–151, 173, 205, 248, 259.

Jenna Agius
Page 135, 260, 264, 270.

Jessica Prescott
Page 92–93, 189, 233, 242–243.

About the author

Gabrielle Nancarrow is a mother of three, an author, a doula and birth educator and the founder of Gather, a space and community for women in Melbourne, Australia. Gabrielle is passionate about supporting families through pregnancy, birth and postpartum and holding space for women as they find their footing on this rocky and wonderful road we call motherhood. This is Gabrielle's second book. She lives with her husband and children in Melbourne.

www.gabriellenancarrow.com

Published in 2023 by Hardie Grant Books, an imprint of Hardie Grant Publishing

Hardie Grant Books (Melbourne)
Wurundjeri Country
Building 1, 658 Church Street
Richmond, Victoria 3121

Hardie Grant Books (London)
5th & 6th Floors
52–54 Southwark Street
London SE1 1UN

hardiegrant.com/books

Hardie Grant acknowledges the Traditional Owners of the Country on which we work, the Wurundjeri People of the Kulin Nation and the Gadigal People of the Eora Nation, and recognises their continuing connection to the land, waters and culture. We pay our respects to their Elders past and present.

A catalogue record for this book is available from the National Library of Australia

The Motherhood Space
ISBN 978 1 74379 854 6

10 9 8 7 6 5 4 3 2 1

Publisher: Alice Hardie-Grant
Managing Editor: Loran McDougall
Project Editor: Antonietta Melideo
Editor: Rochelle Fernandez
Design Manager: Kristin Thomas
Designer: Vanessa Masci
Production Manager: Todd Rechner

Colour reproduction by Splitting Image Colour Studio
Printed in China by Leo Paper Products LTD.

The paper this book is printed on is from FSC®-certified forests and other sources. FSC® promotes environmentally responsible, socially beneficial and economically viable management of the world's forests.